Praise for
Engage, Connect, Protect

Angelou Ezeilo with Nick Chiles offers an accessible guide to respond to the inequities faced by persons of color marginalized by mainstream environmentalism. All of the chapters provide invaluable tools including "Activating a New Generation." Readers have practical tools for doing diverse environmental work.
— Rev. Dr. Dianne Glave, author, *Rooted in the Earth: Reclaiming the African American Environmental Heritage*

Engage, Connect, Protect challenges hypocrisies and challenges all of us in positions of leadership — from the private, public, and social profit sectors — to get comfortable with looking in the mirror to open doors and create cultures where underrepresented people can be vulnerable, authentic, and can feel...safe. Part memoir, part history lesson, part manifesto, this work highlights the cultural connection to nature that black and brown people have always had, and the need, for the sake of our physical, mental, and spiritual health, for it to be reclaimed.
— Kamilah Martin, Global Youth Educator and Vice President at the Jane Goodall Institute

As climate change and race dominate the national dialogue in the United States, Angelou Ezeilo's *Engage, Connect, Protect* is right on time. Ms. Ezeilo artfully articulates the obscured problem of racism in the country's environmental movement and unapologetically sets forth solutions that loom to benefit all of us and the planet.
— Elaine Brown, author, *The Condemnation of Little B* and *A Taste of Power*, slated for film production by Robbie Brenner Productions and Netflix, Fall 2019.

ENGAGE, PROTECT, CONNECT

ENGAGE, CONNECT, PROTECT

Empowering Diverse Youth
as Environmental Leaders

ANGELOU EZEILO
with **NICK CHILES**

Keith —
Thank you for your
commitment to the outdoors!

new society
PUBLISHERS

Cover design by Diane McIntosh. Cover image background (forest): ©iStock; Inset photo: Greening Youth Foundation Achives.
Chapter title image (trees): ©MJ Jessen

Printed in Canada. First printing November 2019.

Inquiries regarding requests to reprint all or part of *Engage, Connect, Protect* should be addressed to New Society Publishers at the address below.
To order directly from the publishers, please call toll-free (North America) 1-800-567-6772, or order online at www.newsociety.com

Any other inquiries can be directed by mail to:
New Society Publishers
P.O. Box 189, Gabriola Island, BC V0R 1X0, Canada
(250) 247-9737

LIBRARY AND ARCHIVES CANADA CATALOGUING IN PUBLICATION

Title: Engage, connect, protect : empowering diverse youth as environmental leaders / Angelou Ezeilo with Nick Chiles.
Names: Ezeilo, Angelou, 1965- author. | Chiles, Nick, author.

Description: Includes index.
Identifiers: Canadiana (print) 2019015439X | Canadiana (ebook) 20190154403 | ISBN 9780865719187
   (softcover) | ISBN 9781550927115 (PDF) | ISBN 9781771423076 (EPUB)

Subjects: LCSH: Environmentalism. | LCSH: Green movement. | LCSH: Environmental management. | LCSH:
   Environmental education. | LCSH: Minorities—Vocational guidance. | LCSH: Minority youth—Conduct of life. | LCSH: Leadership.
Classification: LCC GE195 .E94 2019 | DDC 333.72—dc23

Funded by the Government of Canada
Financé par le gouvernement du Canada
Canada

New Society Publishers' mission is to publish books that contribute in fundamental ways to building an ecologically sustainable and just society, and to do so with the least possible impact on the environment, in a manner that models this vision.

MIX
Paper from responsible sources
FSC
www.fsc.org
FSC® C016245

Certified
B Corporation

new society
PUBLISHERS

Contents

Acknowledgments

THIS BOOK IS DEDICATED to my late Grandma Aline. So much of who I am is because of you. I love you. Your Lula-Belle!

Thank you to my sons, Miles and Cole, for blessing me with the precious gift of motherhood. I love you both to the moon and back — then back again. I have no doubt the world will know your names — not just because I talk about you all of the time. (Ha-ha!)

To my rock, my heartbeat, my partner in life… James. Thank you for saying yes to the Greening Youth Foundation (GYF) experiment some 13 years ago. We knew the road was not going to be easy, but you never doubted me. I love you.

Mom and Dad, thank you for buying those 54 acres in Upstate NY. I truly believe that my life was transformed in those woods. And, as I mature, I see so much of each of you in me: your entrepreneurial passion, love for black people, and love for family. Thank you for being my toughest critics and pushing me to be my best self. Your unconditional love allows me to keep fighting for what I know is right.

Nick, my brother, my ACE, my writing partner. It is no wonder to me that my first book is co-authored with you. As far back as I could remember (all my life), you have been by my side cheering me on. Thank you for helping me pen my life journey to date. To my Sisi, my best friend, aka my big sister. Thank you for always being that sage listener. I am so in debt to you for all of my counseling sessions. Wine credit?

To my stellar GYF family: Ruth and Mike, you two trusted the vision and gave your time and love for the cause so selflessly — thank you. Cameron, although you are one of the newest members to the GYF team, I want to thank you for all of the hours of research you put into this book. To all of our brilliant staff — I know you could be working somewhere else for more money; thank you for your commitment to ensuring that diverse youth have an equitable opportunity to work in the environmental sector. You all rock!

To my fabulous Spelman sisters, keep agitating and changing every damn system! Love y'all!

To Audrey and Frank Peterman, Iantha Wright, Rue Mapp, Dr. Carolyn Finney, Jose Gonzales, Teresa Baker, Maite Acre, Loretta Pineda, and all of the other veterans out there working tirelessly to connect people of color to the outdoors. Thank you for allowing me to lean on you when things seem insurmountable. I also want to thank the next generation of soldiers for joining the movement despite the glaring obstacles.

Lastly, thank you Ashoka and Rachel's Network for providing me the platform and bullhorn to share the GYF story with the world!

CHAPTER 1

The New Paradigm for Environmental Consciousness

I T WAS THE WARMTH AND KINDLINESS of old black ladies that first opened my eyes to the dangerous distance between people of color and the environment.

I was working as a project manager for the Trust for Public Land (TPL), first in New Jersey and then in Atlanta, GA. It was the late 1990s and early 2000s, and my job was to go into certain communities and negotiate land acquisition deals with homeowners in an effort to create more public green space. TPL would then transfer the ownership of the land to local municipalities and governments to create parks and trails, etc. Back in the '90s (before Google Maps!), I would consult physical maps to find the lands that would need to be acquired. I would then go out to various neighborhoods to secure the properties from the homeowners. In other words, I often had to use persuasive tactics to get people to sell their land for the public good. Sometimes it was just a slice of their land, which wouldn't require them to move; other times it was the entire parcel. Of course, I was offering money, but my mandate was to try to get the property as cheaply as possible — the bargain sale.

As we all know, land is one of the Earth's least replenishable commodities. We're not getting any more of it. Everybody's always fighting to get that last piece — usually a battle between public green space developers and commercial building developers. I experienced this dichotomy working for the State of New Jersey Department of Agriculture, specifically the State Agriculture Development Committee. New Jersey was way ahead of its time: In the late '90s, I went to work every day in a state-owned electric car, then visited farmland across south Jersey, negotiating transferred development rights (TDRs) for farmers who were experiencing financial hardship. Most of these farmers were on the brink of selling their precious land to developers in exchange for cash. Therefore, giving them cash in exchange for their development rights on portions of the land was a win-win situation. I had a sense of urgency about the work because I knew if I didn't get there first, the land could be lost to yet another rapacious builder devouring land for profit.

But early on, I realized I had a problem. I was about 30 years old working at TPL, but I probably looked like I was barely in my 20s. In many of the neighborhoods where we were seeking land, the home-owners were primarily African American. This was especially apparent when I moved to Atlanta in 2005 and was working to acquire the land that would become the popular Beltline, the 22-mile abandoned railroad that rings the city. This was also the case while working for the PATH Foundation to negotiate easements for multi-use trails. Many of these neighborhoods were majority black, where I'd knock on the door time and again and find myself facing an older black woman who looked like my grandmother. The second they saw my face, they had immediate trust; I probably reminded them of a daughter or niece. After I got inside, I'd see that smile of familiarity, of comfort, of trust, spread across their face.

In my mind we were supposed to be engaged in a hard-nosed, bare-knuckles negotiation. The kind of negotiating I was trained to do in law school. But there I was sitting across from my grandmother. Law school didn't train me for that. I would explain what was going on, why we were interested in their land, and at first I'd get a lot of quizzical stares. "Wait, you want to do what, baby?" They had no clue what I was talking about, nor any idea that they were sitting on land that could potentially be valuable.

They'd tell me, "Oh baby, whatever you think I need to do, you go ahead and do that." I'd be thinking, Noooooo! I need to negotiate against you!

After all, my job was to get the land for under the market value, ideally for bargain-basement prices. That's certainly what the non-profit organization, the Trust for Public Land, was looking for, what they've been trying to do since their founding in 1972, two years after I was born. But these older black women were so instinctively trusting of me, almost immediately warm and affectionate toward me, that they were not providing me with the adversary I felt like I needed — for their own protection. If they just gave me what I wanted, had I stepped across some kind of ethical line? That was my constant worry. It created a weird dynamic that I was very uncomfortable with. I'd sometimes even ask them if there was somebody else in their lives who could speak on their behalf, like a daughter or nephew somewhere who handled their affairs. If they told me there was, I'd call up that person and hope to negotiate with them. Maybe I'd get a tougher adversary — one that could get them what the land was actually worth.

But throughout the entire encounter, I would realize they had absolutely no idea what was going on, what kind of value they had on their hands. Most of them didn't follow the news reports or the talk in the business world about what was in store for their neighborhood. The savvier ones would figure out that their land was in the middle of something big that was pending, and they'd provide more difficult negotiations. And then there were the speculators and the developers, who would often be trying to get the land before we did. If they could acquire it first, we'd have to buy the land from them. For our purposes, that was the worst-case scenario. It got to the point where organizations like TPL that acquired land decided to stop publishing their proposed land use plans because it got too difficult to complete projects without having to spend far beyond their budgets for acquisition.

Eventually I decided the dynamic for me in these land acquisition negotiations was too much; I left that job. But on my way out, I realized that I was in a unique position to do something about the information deficit I was observing. I needed to find a way to educate the people in these African American communities about the importance of preserving land and about their inadequate access to public parks, particularly for their children. Thankfully, PATH Foundation gave me the opportunity to work as a consultant as I began to think about how I could do something about this glaring problem.

I was tired of the dissonance I would feel when I'd walk into meetings concerning the environment or farmland preservation and be the only black person in the room. All eyes would turn toward me and linger. I knew what everyone was thinking: What are *you* doing here? Eventually I started asking myself the same question: What *am* I doing here? I distinctly remember being in meetings and having out-of-body experiences, looking at myself, wondering: Is there a purpose for you being in this room with all of these white folks? They clearly don't want you here.

However, I knew that unless we started early in teaching young people of color about the importance of being stewards of the Earth, it would be too late by the time they became adults and the imbalances I witnessed would continue. I looked around and saw that no one was teaching this to black and Latino kids — not to mention Native American children. We all have to live on this planet, and we all care about preserving it, so why was it seen as an issue just for wealthy white people? And then I cast my mind back to law school, and how incensed I was as a Fellow at the Center for Governmental Responsibility, learning about environmental justice issues, such as how wastewater treatment plants, sewage plants, and landfills were disproportionately located in communities of color across the US. The environment was incredibly relevant to black people in so many ways.

That's how the Greening Youth Foundation (GYF) was born, through my revelation that my people were the victims of a massive information gap. The environment wasn't just a white issue, and it was about more than saving polar bears or melting ice caps. There were a multitude of environmental issues right here in front of us — and if we were going to make change, we had to stop operating in these segregated silos and bring everyone into the conversation.

It started on Earth Day 2008, at Brookwood Elementary, the elementary school my sons, Miles and Cole, were attending in Gwinnett County, Georgia, a suburb about 40 minutes east of Atlanta. It's astounding to me when I think back over the past decade to recall that my now-global, multimillion-dollar nonprofit started at a class with a couple of dozen five-year-olds. The after-school environmental club, which my father dubbed EcoForce (cool, right?), consisted of a bunch of energetic, mostly white schoolchildren who quickly bought into the idea that protecting and preserving their environment was in their hands. They were willing and eager "stewards." They scoured the school to make sure teachers and classes were recycling all relevant materials, such as paper. They immediately went home and got their parents and families on board. The support we got from the school community was quick and incredibly encouraging. Moms and dads wanted to know what they could do to help the EcoForce club in whatever way they could. They told me their kids banned them from using plastic bags at the supermarket; the little ones would chastise them when they failed to bring reusable bags.

During one of our routine walks, I asked my neighbor, Ruth Kitchen, a lovely and talented white woman who also happened to be a

Ruth Kitchen and Angelou Ezeilo with first GYF environmental education class. CREDIT: GREENING YOUTH FOUNDATION ARCHIVES

teacher, to help me create a K–6 curriculum that schools could utilize to teach children about the importance of them becoming stewards of the Earth. We incorporated music, art, games — our focus was to make it accessible to children by making it fun. When we went into elementary schools in Gwinnett, we were so thrilled to see the curriculum working. The kids were naturally drawn to the message and the call to action. I knew I was on to something.

At this time, we asked my husband, James, who had a thriving law practice in Newark, New Jersey, to help us establish the best legal structure for this new birth we now called Greening Youth Foundation. We also asked a neighborhood friend, Mike Fynn, an engineer, to join our volunteer team. At the time, Mike was appropriately deemed our Technical Director as he would go into schools where the EcoForce clubs were conducting recycling audits. He would break each school into quadrants — participating students would be responsible for promoting recycling in their specific quadrant — and see how effective the club was in reducing waste. James, being the master negotiator, led our negotiations with a recycling company that would come to the school and retrieve the recyclable materials, weigh them, and report back to the school and the students how much trash was diverted from the landfills through their efforts. We would deliver a report card to each school, which excited the young people to no end. They were hyper-motivated to get a good grade on the report card — a concept they knew all too well.

We ran into an obstacle that illustrated just how difficult it would be to truly bring about a change in thinking. The school district had already negotiated contracts with waste removal companies — so even though we were trying to help them save money, they saw little benefit from our efforts. "Eh, we already negotiated the rate with them," was their response.

But we could see that the young people were feeling empowered, realizing that even elementary schoolchildren in a Georgia suburb could help save their planet. We even brought in celebrities to ratchet up the excitement level. Ovie Mughelli, who was an All-Pro fullback for the Atlanta Falcons at the time, was a huge supporter of our efforts, making numerous trips to elementary schools to encourage their recycling efforts. Our big culminating event was the Earth Day Fun Festival. It included recycling parades that featured throngs of children dressed in adorable costumes they had created with recaptured recycled materials, environmentally focused vendors, old-school games, rides, and food. It was a hit. We had done it — children were being environmentally aware while having fun.

It was all good, all encouraging, giving our team of four and the volunteers (Christy Kearney stands out in particular) who were helping us all kinds of warm feelings about the work we were doing. But I soon realized that, to a large extent, I was working with the same population that had always been perceived as the environmental activists — well-to-do white folks. After all, the reason I had decided to throw myself into this project was because of what I had seen in the poorer Atlanta and New Jersey neighborhoods where the residents looked like me. I was grateful for the reception I had gotten in Gwinnett, but if I was really going to activate my mission and start changing the paradigm of who knows about and who cares about the environment, I knew I needed to go back to those Atlanta neighborhoods.

It wasn't very long after we started presenting our curriculum in Atlanta that we realized we had made a mistake in not taking a fresh look at the materials we had created. Ruth is as earnest and excited about this as they come, but as she stood in front of the classroom strumming an acoustic guitar and singing to a room full of black kids, they stared at her with a quizzical, bemused look on their faces. Some of them looked at me, as if to say *Really?* I felt a jolt of panic. This was not going to work for them. I was making the same miscalculation that schools had been making with black and brown kids for decades: not assessing whether the material had any cultural relevancy for them. By using a white woman playing an acoustic guitar and curriculum materials that didn't include illustrations of brown children, I was telling them that I didn't care enough about them and their culture to tailor materials to them. It was certainly what they were used to — but it was not a recipe for success in getting black children to take the material seriously.

Ruth and I went back to my dining room table and redid the curriculum materials. We changed the name of our central character, a detective investigating environmental questions, from Dolly to Dina, one that was a bit more culturally ambiguous. Instead of the acoustic guitar, we played hip-hop, neo-soul, and R&B music and incorporated the latest dances. We were telling the kids that we saw them; they were important. Making those cultural changes was so critical — it made a huge difference in our ability to reach the kids.

Over the past three decades, the environmental community has been dealing with a schism that has created two warring camps: black vs. white; environmental justice vs. conservation; upper-middle-class vs. poor (which usually means black, brown, and Native American). Two separate silos, warily watching each other, judging each other. But if we're really going to make change, we must have both sides dealing with both issues, fighting together. We can no longer afford this polarization and tunnel vision. The climate crisis is something that affects everyone; it's not an issue just for rich white folks. After all, studies have shown that when things like coastal flooding happen, communities of color around the world are more negatively affected. When a nasty storm rumbles into their town, they often don't have the resources to evacuate. They don't have the transportation or the money to live in a hotel somewhere or stay with relatives in a big house away from the danger. We really need to be more holistic in our view and approach to these issues.

I hate when someone introducing me says GYF is tackling environmental justice issues. That's not all we do by a long shot, but too many people when they see brown faces are trained to automatically think it's an environmental justice organization. I think it's somewhat condescending for both sides to think white people only care about polar bears and black people only care about environmental justice. Isn't it all about justice? We also care about the state of the planet. And I know plenty of white people who care about environmental dangers disproportionately burdening communities of color. You can look at the way votes break down on environmental questions and bond referenda at the ballot box to see that, when asked, black and brown communities will vote overwhelmingly in favor of protecting the planet and creating more green spaces. In some ways, the voting on election day is often the purest way to assess how communities of color feel about these issues because typically they are confronting those ballot questions for the first time and haven't encountered fliers from the Democratic and Republican parties telling them how to vote. No, it's just that voting lever and their conscience and priorities at work. I'm well-versed on the major environmental questions of the day, but sometimes even I have to read through the question several times to understand what it's asking. Without prepping from my political party of choice, I have to dig down and assess how I actually feel about the issue. It's too late to consult Google to see how the liberals or conservatives are telling me to vote. Only in recent years has the data been aggregated to show that people of color are huge supporters and protectors of the environment. I find that information to be extremely empowering. You can no longer tell me I only care about food, housing, and education because of my skin color. That's the message I have gotten for too many years: Oh, the state of the planet isn't your issue, let us worry about that. You keep fighting poverty and racism. Now we are announcing to the world, Yes, we *do* care about where the park will be located and the healthiness of our food.

The next phase for GYF came when we realized that we could not only train youth of color to be stewards of the environment but also lead them into actual careers in the environment: engaging, important careers that could sustain them for the rest of their lives, in an area that had traditionally been shut off to people of color. This work has brought us some of our greatest successes as an organization; former GYF interns are serving as park rangers across the nation, or doing critical work in other sectors of the natural resource management field.

Frankly, it is through the environmental internships and careers that I have been able to get a lot of environmental justice folks interested in the work that GYF does. If I say, Look at the enormous disparities in the racial breakdown of environmental careers, I'll immediately have their attention. They see that there are justice questions at play over here as well. When it comes to internships and careers, it's all a question of access. Once you give youth of color access to this world and show them what's possible, they jump at the chance. I understand that because it happened to me as well. As a student, I had no idea these were fields I could pursue. I went into law, the logical end result in my mind of the path laid before me throughout my schooling. It was part of the equation for a girl from a solid middle-class black family: a good education leading to a good job and a good career. Environmentalism was quite far from my post-secondary radar screen. I'm not even sure how my parents would have reacted if my 23-year-old self had pronounced that I was going to be an environmental attorney.

With our students, the words of the astronaut/teacher Sally Ride apply quite profoundly: "You gotta see it to be it." First you must have access to it for you to know it even exists. Once you see it but you don't see anybody who looks like you doing it, it likely won't resonate with you. When we get our interns working in national forests and national parks giving them exposure to careers in natural resource management, they quickly become models to the people visiting the parks. Last summer, through a program birthed in 2012 by my husband James and George McDonald — the Youth Program Director (now more aptly called a friend) at the National Park Service (NPS) — called HBCUI (Historically Black Colleges and Universities Internship program), we had 50 interns working in national parks where African Americans have left indelible contributions. Places like Tuskegee National Historic Site and Martin Luther King Jr. National Historical Park, and some of the country's most popular national parks, such as Yellowstone, Yosemite, Grand Canyon, and the Everglades. Millions of visitors, including many children, passed through those parks during the summer, each of them observing brown people working at the sites. That single encounter changed or formed each child's view of who could work in those places — the green and gray uniform of the NPS reflecting back a

Nicole McHenry, National Park Service; George McDonald, National Park Service; Angelou Ezeilo and James Ezeilo, Greening Youth Foundation, at HBCUI 2018 Career and Leadership Workshop in Tuskegee, AL.
CREDIT: EBONI PRESTON

gleam in the eye of that child of color who, perhaps much to his parents' dismay, just happens to love working outdoors with plants and animals. A decade or two later, this encounter could result in that child donning the NPS uniform himself, pursuing a career working with endangered species, or maybe ecology or botany.

I have to address here an issue that I've discovered over the last couple of decades working in the environmental space. For many black people, especially older generations, the outdoors conjures a lot of historical negativity that they'd rather forget — merciless toil in endless fields under a brutal sun; night riders wielding shotguns and menace; rapes and lynchings possibly waiting at the next curve in the road. Even before our ancestors were brought here shackled in the holds of ships, in West Africa we traded stories of scary beings in the woods, keeping many people from venturing outside at night. Many of these myths and stories are still told in Africa and in the Caribbean. This unrest and fear sits in our bones like a congenital disease, to be foisted onto the next generation. Carolyn Finney, a professor at the University of Kentucky, persuasively probed this phenomenon in her 2014 book, *Black Faces, White Spaces: Reimagining the Relationship of African Americans to the Great Outdoors*. Finney claims that the legacies of slavery, Jim Crow, and racial violence have shaped our cultural understanding of the outdoors and our view of who should and can have access to natural spaces.

We see this every year with each new group of interns, hear it in the voices of their parents when they're asking us questions about their children's safety in these far-flung parks surrounded by white people. We have their babies, and we're sending them to places they've never been before themselves. They call us and say, "Is my baby safe? Are they going to be okay?" In some of these parks, there's virtually no cell phone coverage, so they can't get hourly check-ins once their child is gone. We find ourselves doing a lot of counseling and consoling with the parents. In effect, we're rewriting that family's entire idea of the outdoors as a dangerous space, shifting the paradigm completely by saying it's okay to be in those places. As of 2018, we had sent more than 5,000 interns into national parks and forests across the country, and wonderfully, easily 85 percent of them reported having positive experiences. Many of them now even bring their families back and have picnics with their parents and their aunties and their grandparents. They send us pictures all the time. Their decision to become interns through GYF has a mushrooming effect on everyone in their lives, rippling outward and touching black folks across the land.

I understand the apprehension of the parents. It comes from not knowing, from their unfamiliarity with these outdoor places and spaces. With two children of my own, I know it's a parent's job to be leery of the unknown even when your child is moving blissfully ahead without a care — sometimes you're leery *because* your child is blissfully uncaring. After the internship is over, many parents are not entirely comfortable with their child announcing that they want to pursue an environmental career, thinking: Is that good and stable enough?

Can you make enough money doing that? That's why the exposure and education are crucial for everybody in the community. We need to send out the word that careers in natural resource management can be added to the list of good stable jobs.

It has been interesting for us to see that these federal land management agencies need us perhaps even more than we need them. For too long, they were focused on one demographic: middle-class white males. But now those long-time white male rangers are retiring and the agencies are having a difficult time finding enough candidates to fill their positions. The National Park Service, Forest Service, Bureau of Land Management, and other federal land management agencies are discovering all of this hidden talent among young people they never before considered. Through GYF, they have tapped into a new well-spring. The agencies are thrilled to find out that these young people are fantastic workers. We know because after a summer with GYF interns they call us back and eagerly ask for more. For instance, we partnered with organizations in the West that fight forest fires because we were interested in showing them that African American males are ideal for hiring. Many of the guys (in some cases, ladies) from some of the toughest neighborhoods in the country were perfect workers for the task at hand: ambitious, athletic, and fearless.

Of late, we have set our sights on another lily-white corner of the environmental world: the outdoor retailer industry. These companies have long been connected to federal land management agencies because they provide gear that outdoor enthusiasts and workers need when toiling outside in all kinds of conditions. If you look around at the workforce of these companies, you see the same homogeneity that plagued the federal agencies. Their demographics were a perfect mirror of each other, except one was private and one was public. The retailers are driven by an added incentive that doesn't enter into the federal agency picture: the profit motive. They are eager to sell their wares to large and growing demographics that they hadn't yet connected with, namely communities of color. But it seems they hadn't realized that if they wanted to sell to these communities, perhaps it might be helpful to employ some of their members. At least that's me giving them the benefit of the doubt. It seems they hadn't yet made this connection, though it's always possible that they just weren't interested in hiring members of these communities. I have to admit I am still stunned by how overwhelmingly white these companies are at this rather late date, closing in on 2020. We have been in discussions with their representatives about creating internships to include young people of color. Progress has been slow but steady. Admittedly it is not easy, but we all must try a little harder — after all, it has taken decades to create the scenario we have today. Some companies that are new to the scene, like Wylder Goods, inherently get it. Other more established ones, like the North Face, are starting to make more of the connection. These companies understand the economic and social benefits of diversity and inclusivity.

It's fascinating because if you polled the executives from this industry, a vast majority of them would probably consider themselves to be politically liberal and aware. To use a popular term, they might consider themselves *woke*. But somehow they forgot to apply that liberalism to their workforce. I get it — kinda. It's comfortable to be surrounded by people who look like you, who think like you, who like the same food, the same music. It's easy. It's more work to include people who may have different preferences for food, music, and vacation destinations.

I had an extremely unsettling experience when I attended a retreat for the Trust for Public Land out in Sonoma County, California. One early morning, a colleague and I decided to take a walk. In an attempt to get some exercise, we were briskly walking down the street from our hotel, enjoying the lovely surroundings, deep in conversation about our personal lives and our families. Out of nowhere, a white woman drove by in a Ford Element SUV (orange; I will never forget that color) and shouted, "Go home!" I was stunned. Napa Valley's beauty instantly turned ugly and sinister. When I got back to the retreat and reported what had happened, my co-workers were somewhat surprised. But I needed to get out of there. I called my husband immediately because the plan was for him to meet me in Napa Valley for a mini-vacation. However, I wanted no part of the place, so I packed my bags and within a couple of hours was headed to the airport to fly back to Atlanta. I later told my colleagues that they need to think very hard about the kinds of places we go for our retreats in the future — and of course this area in Sonoma County should be snatched off the list immediately. Their response? Blah, blah, blah. A lot of lip service. But the point is that they now needed to start considering such issues so that someone like me could be as comfortable as they were.

I know this part of the story gets really complicated. See, TPL has a great mission of conserving land for the public. In fact, I am appreciative of TPL, because I found them after working for the government, which I knew was not the answer for me. The national NGO really gave me my wings and perspective, and I will always be thankful. However, working for them and other environmental NGOs also emphasized the incredible polarity that exists in the conservation world. Particularly, I got a certain understanding of the white liberal world. Whenever things would get racially uncomfortable at the workplace, it would often be written off as an exaggerated aberration: "Surely you misunderstood his/her intention ..." or "Let's not lose sight of the issue at hand."

It was very frustrating navigating the workplace environment because I knew race was always something people did *not* want to discuss. But, how could we ever move beyond the discomfort if no one was willing to talk about it? My most hated phrase was "Angelou, I don't even see color — we all look the same." Really? In short, I knew I needed to leave this work world so that I could actually breathe. Most importantly, I wanted to make sure that no young brown person in the future with an interest in an environmental field had to exist in this schizophrenic workplace.

But I know I can't present an angry face to the world. I've spent too many years of my adult life observing the peril that angry black women encounter in professional spaces. Often we encounter the same peril whether we're angry or not. I can be literally melting inside from the angry heat I'm feeling, but I know I must keep it hidden. They don't want to see Angry Angelou. She won't help anybody. I know I have to present Smiling Angelou. She makes big moves. I can't say to them,

"You know what? It's 2017 and everyone in this room is white! You don't see a problem with that?" Even if I'm thinking that, it has to come out like this: "I understand that you looked up and realized you weren't being as intentional about diversity as you needed to be and about having other perspectives around the table. Okay, so let me help you be more representative of the world we all live in."

It reminds me of scenes from the television show *Black-ish* with Anthony Anderson and Tracee Ellis Ross. They do a great job of depicting the comfort that white characters have around each other at the advertising agency where Anthony's character works — and the unease they have talking about anything related to race. It might be comedy, but for many African Americans who work around white people, unfortunately those scenes are all too real. That's what drives many of us out of corporate America and turns us into entrepreneurs — exhaustion, frustration, resignation.

I was proud when a group of GYF interns learned very early that they didn't necessarily need corporate America. We had trained these young adults in our Urban Youth Corps to work in urban agriculture and landscape management, but when they finished the program, they couldn't get jobs. Although this demographic was receiving incredible training and certifications in various areas, not many sectors had actual jobs waiting for them. So, in many cases, these young adults didn't stop there; they created their own businesses. They said we have the skill set now, so why are we waiting to get hired? There are reams of data showing that entrepreneurship among African American women is flying off the charts. This feeling of us not being included or accepted is giving birth to wonderful new businesses.

We know that much of this is slow work, transforming one person, one company, one neighborhood at a time. For instance, I'm seeing the black community beginning to embrace the idea and necessity of healthy eating. When I was on a panel, I heard someone say, "Healthy people are happy people — and happy people want to make the world a better place." I got excited about that line. Black communities are beginning to insist that they have access to locally grown food. It's becoming chic to have a plant-based diet. If they still eat beef, they are insisting that it be farm-raised and organic. Sometimes I have thrilling little moments when I know it's working, transforming lives. A decade ago, one of my family elders used to tease me about my vegetarian diet. At family functions, he'd look at my plate and say, "What you eatin', grass?" He'd walk off, laughing real hard at his little joke. At a recent family gathering, he said, "Angelou, I'm eating like you now." Well into his eighth decade, he had made the connection between his diet and his health. He's nearly a vegetarian now. I told him, "Now this is a moment."

Why would people of color conclude that they don't want to feel well? Now you see urban agriculture blossoming in our neighborhoods, black people going back to their roots, wanting to see their vegetables growing out of the ground. I joke that we've always been proponents of the "slow food" movement, long before it had a name. We did it out of necessity. Now we're returning to this lifestyle, recognizing that many issues plaguing our youth, such as obesity and diabetes, can be traced directly to fast food, to McDonald's Happy Meals and a KFC two-piece-and-a-biscuit.

If our next generation can become more aware of the importance of locally grown food on good soil with no pesticides, it will result in us all living longer, happier, healthier lives. That's a movement we can all get behind.

CHAPTER 2

Environmental Jargon Creates Exclusion

IT WAS IN FRONT OF the roughest audience imaginable — a classroom of fifth graders — that I discovered how painfully exclusive is the language we typically use in the green space. Talk about your tough crowds. I was at an Atlanta elementary school with Ruth Kitchen, our educational director at the time. We figured we would start off as we usually did, by trying to get the students to interact with us. So, we asked the class who among them would consider themselves "environmentalists." This room full of about two dozen African American 10-year-olds looked at us like we had three heads and six eyes. These students had signed up to be part of our EcoForce club, so we knew they were already interested in the environment. But the question was not registering with them at all. Ruth and I looked at each other, brows furrowed. To understand the extreme panic that coursed through my brain, you should recognize how much time and energy had been directed up to that point in creating this curriculum and approach. It had worked so well in Gwinnett, we had been so thoroughly congratulated for our efforts, that we walked into that classroom supremely confident of our methods. But it didn't take long at all for our confidence to be shattered. If you have stood in front of a classroom of skeptical fifth graders well on their way to exhibiting their boredom and maybe even lack of respect, you will know exactly what we were feeling. If you haven't, try to imagine what it might feel like for a comedian to realize *nobody* is laughing at her jokes — and she still has a half hour to go in the set. I'm not embarrassed to say that a layer of sweat began to form on my forehead. I'm sure Ruth was experiencing the same thing. Fifth graders can smell fear and panic like hyenas. I knew I had to pull it together real fast.

"Who likes to be able to go outside and play?" I asked them. Of course, they all raised their hands.

"Who likes the fact that they have a park near their house to play basketball and get on the swings and slides?" Ruth asked, immediately knowing where I was going with this line of questioning. The hands all went up again.

"Who likes to be able to go to the sink, turn on the faucet and get a glass of water they can drink?" All hands went up.

"How many of you have asthma or have friends who do?" A sea of hands. That one really hit me hard.

"Wouldn't it be great if you could go outside and breathe the air and not have to worry about the breathing machine?" I asked. "Who likes fresh air?"

We went on and on, talking about food, asking them if they were glad they could buy fresh fruit and vegetables at the supermarket. Being 10-year-olds, when they heard the word "vegetables," we got a chorus of "Ewww!" But they got the point.

"Everything you just agreed to means that each of us is an environmentalist," we told them.

For too many kids of color, that classroom episode wasn't a rarity — they're used to being force-fed curriculum that was not designed to touch them. I can certainly remember that experience in my own childhood, when I'd have to memorize material that was so far from my own interests and life that it would be much more difficult for me to make the essential connections that white children had a much easier time with. And the way that education has worked in America in the decades since integration, the teachers and the school will focus on deficits in the students when they don't quickly master the material. What's wrong with these kids? Maybe it's their home environments, or their parents, or their lack of money, or — yes, I'm going there — their skin color?

As Ruth and I stood there in front of the class and were devastated to discover that we had made the same mistake that school systems had been making for far too long with kids of color, we could have walked away drawing the same conclusions that schools had made for the last couple of generations: these kids can't get it because something is wrong with them. But instinctively we knew that wasn't the right conclusion to draw. No, the problem was with *us*, not with them. When we drew up the lesson plans and created the materials, we had not seen them. So, we had to quickly figure out a way to connect with these kids so that they would understand the point of the information we were trying to impart. We had to be nimble, flexible—to put aside our carefully laid plans, even if they represented many hours of work. And even — and this is so vital a point — if those plans had already worked in Gwinnett County with a different population of children. In many ways, this is a microcosm of the point of this entire book: just because a particular method might have worked in the past and with a particular population doesn't mean that it's going to continue to work. And the onus is on you to recognize when it's no longer working and figure out a new approach.

This wasn't a problem a generation before me, when my parents were attending all-black elementary schools enforced by legal segregation. They were taught by caring and compassionate black teachers who usually instinctively knew how to cater lessons to their students. But then the US Supreme Court in the 1954 *Brown v. Board of Education of Topeka* decision mistook the demands of the plaintiffs for equal schools and deemed that equality meant they needed to sit next to white students. As a result, many all-black schools across America were shut down, and an estimated 50,000 black teachers were fired, leaving us with the school configurations we still have today: namely, mostly white teachers instructing black students. Studies have shown that black students in elementary school who have black teachers perform better on standardized tests and face more favorable teacher perceptions. In addition, according to a Johns Hopkins study, low-income black students who have at least one black teacher in elementary school are significantly more likely to graduate from high school and consider attending college. Similarly, it has been shown that black students perform better in HBCUs because they are taught in nuturing environments primarily by teachers that look like them.

But as we have confronted the realization that, for many reasons, we are unlikely to get many more black teachers in America's schools, educators have pushed for something called "culturally relevant instruction," which attempts to take into account the particular culture of the students. This wasn't an issue for us in Gwinnett County, Georgia, when we began. The students were predominantly well-to-do white kids who had a very different base level of knowledge about these environmental issues than did the students in Atlanta. These middle-class students had heard words like "renewables, energy, reduce, reuse, recycle." They might not have known exactly what they all meant, but the concepts the words explored were part of a lexicon to which they had been exposed. Even the word "environmentalist" would resonate with them. They had grown up with these concepts swirling around them. The parents immediately embraced what we were doing; the science teachers quickly saw how our work could complement what was being taught in Natural Science class — a class that you'd be hard-pressed to find in Atlanta.

If we had started out at a more middle-class predominantly black school in Atlanta, perhaps our reception might have been different. But that initial foray into Atlanta took place at a Title I school, which meant that at least 40 percent of the students in the building met the federal definition for low-income. The Title I program has been around for more than 50 years and currently provides more than $14 billion to thousands of schools and more than 6 million students across the country to help offset the negative effects of poverty. The fact that the school was deemed low-income meant that the students were much less likely to have encountered the environmental concepts we expected them to already know.

As I left the classroom that day, it was becoming clearer to me that the jargon, the mindset, the overall approach we use in this field often has the effect of excluding groups of people. I don't think it's necessarily done on purpose, but it's definitely something we need to explore further, to fix. The environmental community must look inward and ask: Why aren't we able to connect with these communities of color? Why aren't they at the table? Where's the disconnect?

We use so many words in the environmental community, words that have become second nature to us, that send very distinct messages to communities sitting outside of our world. For instance, even the word "organic." Let's take a step back and think about how the average person typically encounters that word. If you'd never really paid much attention to the word before, upon a cursory investigation an inescapable fact jumps out at you: organic costs more. And not just a few pennies more, but considerably more — as much as 20 to 100 percent, according to some estimates. Right away, you conclude that "organic" must be some kind of synonym for "rich-people food." For those on a limited budget,

Order of appearance, left to right: Miles, Angelou, Cole, and James at Miles and Mari's high-school graduation party.
Credit: Ezeilo family

they're going to conclude that "organic," whatever it means, is not intended for them. Even before they come across some kind of public education or marketing campaign that explains how organic food is free of harmful pesticides that conglomerates use to enable them to mass produce our food and increase their profits, they are starting from a position of extreme skepticism. Even after they encounter the explanations for the organic price difference, they might conclude that the food they normally eat hasn't hurt them yet so it must be okay — and thus not worth the heftier price tag for the so-called safe food.

For African Americans, the race factor must be added to the equation. It's clearly something for white people, which automatically lets you know it wasn't intended for you. If the pro-organic argument is coming from white people, an enormous amount of racial distrust is overlaid on the issue. We have years, generations, of painful experiences and shocking revelations screaming at us that we can't trust the things white people tell us when it comes to our health. Probably the most infamous was the so-called Tuskegee syphilis experiment, during which the US Public Health Service studied 600 poor sharecroppers in Alabama from 1932 to 1972 to observe the effects of untreated syphilis. The black men were told they were receiving free health care from the United States government, but in fact they were being watched to see what would happen to them if their syphilis was untreated — even after penicillin had become the standard treatment for syphilis by 1947. The men were told that the study was only going to last six months, but it actually lasted 40 years — without them ever being told they had the disease or ever being treated with penicillin. There are many more documented cases of racist treatment by the medical and scientific communities to give black people plenty of reasons for their distrust.

But we don't even need to go that deep to understand why people would turn their backs on organic. We can just stay right there with the pocketbook. It's no shock to note that African Americans are more likely to be grappling with financial challenges. Hispanic Americans too. Money matters. Hell, I've been a vegetarian the majority of my life (thirty-plus years) — and a vegan the last ten years. I make a pretty decent living, but when I go to a Whole Foods or high-end stores like it, I know I can't buy everything organic. I have to make quick calculations about the things I will spend the extra money on because it's so cost prohibitive. I usually stick with the dirty dozen — vegetables whose skin is edible (like cucumbers, squash, broccoli, lettuce) and thus more susceptible to corruption by pesticide. The price tag still hurts, but I know the extra expense is worth it. My eldest son, Miles, prepared me as he was about to head off to Howard University that he will no longer be able to be vegan. Somewhat disappointed, I asked him why. His response was, there is no way he could afford a vegan diet in college. I knew he wasn't wrong. The best bet is to go to a farmers' market, where you know what farm produced the fruits and vegetables and what type of soil and pesticides were used. Buying direct from farms is usually much cheaper than at the large chains; they don't have to think about packaging and how to get it to the distribution centers and so forth. However, I recognize many people don't have access to farmers' markets.

A considerable amount of progress can be made if we think about the mere semantics. Instead of using the word "organic," which is now a word unfortunately associated with rich white people, if we say "locally grown" I think we'd get a very different response in black communities and other communities of color. That gets back to this question of trust — if we are told that the produce is coming from local farms that very well may be black-owned, our entire mindset changes. We'd feel a connection to the food in a much different way. We would trust the food. If we started doing that, perhaps we could attach it to a major public education campaign linking the foods we eat to many of the chronic illnesses that are more prevalent in the black community, like asthma and diabetes and hypertension. If people in lower-income communities knew that the way their food is grown and mass-distributed might be connected to all the diabetes in their family, I know they would make different choices about the food they buy. I think many more people would be willing to pay extra for the clean food, the organic food.

At GYF we have been bringing the entire family into our environmental wellness programs by sending home notes with the children.

We understood quickly that if we're not educating the parents or care-givers, then some of the lessons learned in the classroom are lost. If we are talking about the importance of tote bags instead of plastic bags and how to pack lunches so you don't create as much trash with plastic wrap, if we're not directing the message to the caregivers, how is an 8-year-old or even a teenager going to be able to effect change? We've even tried to use text messages to educate the caregivers, calibrating the most effective way to reach them. I know it's working because we will have parents and grandparents complain to us that their children won't let them get the plastic bags at the grocery store anymore, or the kids insist they put school lunches in reusable Tupperware instead of the wasteful non-biodegradable packaging that clutters landfills.

At times, however, I admit that our efforts have backfired, such as when a caregiver clapped back at us with something like: "I can only buy what's available in our community." She was talking about food deserts — the painful lack of fresh and healthy foods in low-income communities. This is a tragic and well-documented problem in black and latinx communities. In bodegas and grocery stores all across America, the meats, fruits, and vegetables sometimes aren't even the same color as in the stores that serve white neighborhoods. I've seen statistics stating that as many as 23 million Americans live in food des-erts, which is a staggering number. An estimated 1 in 8 Americans face food insecurity, according to the organization Feeding America — and 13 million of them are children.

The comment I got from that caregiver forced me to go back to the drawing board and think more deeply about the messages we were passing along to these children touched by GYF. It's unfair and almost cruel to preach to them about proper food choices if their families don't have access to them. This reminds me of what Mickey Fearn, former deputy director of the National Park Service, once told an audience: When we take children from a poverty-stricken community in the city and expose them to our iconic beautiful national parks, it's almost cruel because they are now acutely aware of what they don't have. And let me not even start on the message we send to black and

Hispanic Americans when gentrification takes hold in their community. Basically, our nation is telling them that they are only deserving of high-quality food if there are white people nearby. It's become a community joke — if they're building a Whole Foods in your neighborhood, you know you're soon going to be forced out by mommies with jogging strollers.

As I noticed when trying to negotiate with elderly black women to buy their lands for New Jersey or Georgia public space, or later on when GYF would communicate with families, the messenger is all-important when it comes to the question of trust. Because of our history, people of color are much quicker to have trust in people who look like them — granted, that can sometimes be to their detriment. But it's a reality that must be taken into consideration by any large-scale movement such as the environmental movement. I'm not saying that you have to be of the same race as the person you're delivering the message to, but when there's a history of distrust built into the community's DNA, having culturally relevant messages and people that can connect to the audience make a world of difference.

It's also not a bad idea to take the community's needs and basic human motivations into consideration when you're trying to change behavior. When I was growing up in the Northeast in the 1970s, I distinctly remember seeing the note on beverage cans and bottles informing consumers that the empty container could actually be exchanged for cash. I remember thinking that a whole nickel for an empty bottle seemed like a pretty good deal; there were quite a few delicious brands of penny candy I could buy for a nickel. After Oregon passed the first bottle bill in 1971, removing about 7 percent of its garbage from the waste stream, other states followed suit, encouraging recycling by giving cash for the empties. I can recall the dudes pushing the shopping carts overflowing with cans and bottles through black neighborhoods, provided a way of earning money while the rest of us perhaps unconsciously served as environmental stewards by recycling. As an adult, I've been disappointed that bottle bills haven't become the national norm; currently only 10 states have container deposit bills. The US beverage industry has concluded that these laws hurt their bottom lines, so they lobby against them. This is especially sad considering the evidence from the 10 states about how effective the laws are: Studies show that total roadside litter was reduced by between 30 percent and 64 percent. In addition, while the nation's overall beverage container recycling rate is approximately 33 percent, states with deposit laws have a 70 percent average rate. When Michigan had a law in place from 1990 to 2008, its recycling rate was an astounding 97 percent — largely attributable to a 10-cent deposit, compared to a nickel everywhere else. As mind-boggling as our current environmental woes are, why not make a strong push to provide incentives for recycling? Some states, like California, do this beautifully. The cash-back incentive allows us to make progress without having to sink into the endless, mind-numbing debates between progressives and conservatives, Democrats and Republicans, blue and red. We don't have time to waste; we must attack this from as many directions as possible.

I know that words like "composting" also have acquired negative connotations for black and Hispanic people, probably because of these communities' histories. Try convincing an elderly black woman that she should leave her food waste outside instead of taking advantage of modern conveniences like trash pickup, and her mind very well may return to her childhood in the South, where predominantly black communities were used as garbage dumps for the disposal of everybody else's waste — a practice that unfortunately still continues across America. Those communities, often blanketed by putrid odors, struggled to stop the dumping of nasty garbage waste outside, and now someone is trying to convince her to do it in her own home, under the guise of helping the environment? She's likely to look at the request as just another inexplicable request from wealthy white folks. It reminds me of the efforts by first-world countries like the US to force developing countries to halt their growth and abide by environmental standards the developed countries are not willing to live by themselves.

One of the most effective ways of filling people with the desire to be protective of natural resources is by getting them outside, in the countryside, in the fresh air, especially in a place where they can truly gawk in wonder at Mother Nature's creations. But just as I finish typing that sentence, I have to confront the follow-up: How much is that going to cost? The entire realm of the outdoors in the US has become tied up in the question of access — are they truly places that all Americans can take advantage of, or are they reserved for the wealthy few, like a vast big sky resort built over thousands of years by wind and rain and floods and earthquakes? When poor people are cut off from visiting our national parks and gazing in amazement at what nature has created, there are consequences. First, these people conclude that these places are not intended for them to enjoy. America has created a system where only the well-to-do experience and benefit from the beauty of our lands. While the fee to enter the park might not be prohibitive, when you factor in the cost to travel to the Grand Canyon or Yellowstone, do a few of the onsite excursions like a jeep tour or mule ride, secure lodging and pay for food, we're talking a bundle of cash. One website I visited put the price tag for a three-day Grand Canyon vacation for a family of four at $4,732. That is far from cheap; hell, you could probably have a fabulous time in Paris or Cape Town at that price. But even when well-to-do people of color have the means to embark on a nature vacation, such an adventure falls so far from their radar screens that it's not something they would ever consider. Three days hiking the Grand Canyon or strolling the vineyards in California? Hmm. In my own experience, when I suggest to black family and friends that they should consider such a trip, I am met with discomfort and a *lot* of questions: Is it safe? Are there any black people there? How will we be treated?

Even if you don't have the problem of a limited budget, if you're going through the trouble of planning out a family vacation, the last thing you want to do is bring your family to a place where you're worried about their treatment. This was the idea behind the *Negro Travelers' Green Book*, which was first published in 1936 by Victor Hugo Green, a New York City mailman. Green, whose first book focused on New York, wanted to give black travelers a reference document they could use to find food and lodging that was relatively friendly to black people. As more blacks joined the middle class and bought cars, this became increasingly necessary. By driving cars, black professionals like athletes, entertainers, and salesmen who spent a lot of time on the road could avoid the unpredictable vagaries of public transportation, which might or might not be racially segregated from city to city — often depending on who was operating the bus or train and who was riding in it. Things were much simpler and less stressful if you could drive your own car, that is, until you needed to stop to eat or sleep.

Even though I was born in 1970, four years after the green book ceased publication — ostensibly, the Civil Rights Act outlawed the segregation of public spaces, meaning black people were supposed to be able to travel freely and sit and eat wherever they wanted — the concept of traveling free of racial discrimination was something that I felt acutely as a child. When I was about 6 years old, my parents decided that we would vacation in a different spot on the Jersey Shore than we normally went. Atlantic City had been our spot in the years before, a place that my family found fairly welcoming and comfortable. The Jersey Shore was notorious for its palpable racism in many beach towns, so black people at the time knew they had to be very careful about where they chose to stay. In the summer of 1977, my parents decided to give Seaside Heights a try. This Ocean County town was a popular destination for many of the white families who lived around us in Jersey City; my older sister and brother and I used to hear white kids talking about it all the time, like it was some magical Narnia-like land of fun and games. But it turned out to be a nightmare for the Chiles family.

There was excitement in the air when we packed up our olive-green family van and pulled away from Pavonia Avenue in Jersey City for our beach vacation. My family has always been a laugh a minute, with my father leading the way with his wicked, dry sense of humor. The jokes were flying high that morning as we hit the Garden State Parkway headed south for Seaside Heights, about 90 minutes away. We were giddy when we crossed the bridge to the Barnegat Peninsula, which sat apart from the mainland on a long stretch alongside the Atlantic

Ocean. We could see the foamy surf washing over the soft inviting sands of Seaside Heights.

My father had picked out a motel that was a coin's toss from the beach, to give us maximum time to romp in the surf and build entire sandcastle cities. I could feel the anticipation racing down my spine. This weekend was going to be a thrill a minute; I just *knew* it. When we pulled up to the motel, only a couple of cars were already in the parking lot, the pink neon "Vacancy" clearly illuminated. We all tumbled out of the van, young bladders relieved that a bathroom was just minutes away. My mother, my siblings, and I followed my dad into the office. We saw a young white woman behind the registration desk. Her eyes appeared to widen as she saw us; this reaction from an adult was not something that would register in my 6-year-old mind.

"We're here to check in," my father said. "The name is Chiles."

"Um, okay, just wait a second," the young woman said. Quickly, she disappeared through a doorway leading to a back office. As we waited, I looked around the lobby. I had always liked hotels and motels; what little kid doesn't? They signify vacations, room service, restaurants or fast-food takeout, and an unending string of fun fun fun. I looked over at my older brother Nick; I could see he shared my excitement.

The young woman came back out, now accompanied by an older white woman. Both of them had strange looks on their faces, like they were about to sit down in a dentist chair for a root canal.

"Um, excuse me, but we don't have any vacancies," the older woman said to my father.

There were several seconds of silence that followed her statement. I wasn't aware of what had just happened, what was the meaning behind the words she said. But my dad and my mom surely did.

"But the vacancy sign is lit up." I think this might have come from my mother.

The older woman shifted her feet. Now she wasn't even looking at us anymore. My family standing in front of her, awaiting our highly anticipated vacation weekend, was a sight that she could no longer stand. She was now speechless.

And so was my father. He didn't say another word to her. I glanced at his face; he wore an expression I had never seen before. In retrospect, his face contained the anguish of generations of his ancestors, that painful ingestion of rage black people have had to force down whenever confronted with the reality of our place in America.

We followed my dad out of the office, back into the olive-green van. It was like the family's elation had been punctured with a pin. We eventually found a motel that agreed to take our legal American tender. But it was too late; the weekend had been destroyed. My father retreated into a shell that weekend; he barely spoke to us and had a difficult time conjuring a smile.

That same pain has been endured by black people in America for years. It was an incident that my siblings and I would carry with us for the rest of our lives. It would always be in the backs of our minds as we considered taking trips to places we didn't know very well, the possibility that a family adventure could quickly turn into nightmare. Black people sometimes joke among ourselves about how we get locked into visiting the same places every year — the same Southern towns, the same Caribbean islands, the same cruise lines. But is it any wonder, with this ugly history lurking just over our shoulder?

For me, fast-forward four decades — decades that included the election of Barack Obama, twice — and there I am in Sonoma County, blissfully walking the streets with a work colleague, as I recounted in the previous chapter. My conference is rudely shattered by a white woman shouting at me to go home. My point is that there needs to be serious contemplation given to the marketing of these important experiences to people of color. The travel and environmental industries need to at least try to assure families that they will be warmly welcomed in America's national parks — and then work hard to make sure that's the case. Once more of us start going, it will have a domino effect throughout the community and many others will follow.

Traveling to these breath-taking sites also has another related benefit. Witnessing the splendor of nature fundamentally changes our relationship to the environment. We become more protective, more solicitous, more apprehensive about damage being visited upon these marvels. When you camp at Yosemite, you make damn sure you leave the campsite exactly as you found it; you don't want to be the one personally responsible for spoiling perfection. When we immerse ourselves in it, drown in its beauty, breathe in the sweetness of the air, we begin to feel personally responsible for what happens to the environment: we become stewards. This stewardship extends back to our own home communities and then spans outward to the rest of the planet. Encouraging someone to recycle or compost or even engage in a protest becomes a lot easier once they have had a personal experience that at times feels almost spiritual. When I'm bearing witness to nature's wonder, I feel like something changes inside of me; it's cathartic every time. The personal connection is much stronger and more immediate than it is if you spend all your days surrounded by concrete and man-made edifices, disconnected from the consequences of your daily decisions regarding environmental stewardship. Once you're connected, that extends to your local park, the lake down the street, the trees in your backyard. You want to protect them, preserve them. You care what happens in every corner of the Earth.

For these reasons, I think getting young people of color to our national parks should be a national priority if we want to cultivate future stewards. That means we need to begin thinking differently about the ways that people of color first encounter the words and the messages the environmental community tosses around, blithely unaware of the consequences. It is imperative that we begin to address exclusion as soon as possible if we're going to turn this around. We exclude at our own peril. In this age, when we are clearly engaged in a battle to the death (literally), we need to conscript every soldier within reach.

Chapter 3

Nature as Healer

I LEARNED ABOUT the incredible healing power of nature in the most personal and traumatic of ways. In this chapter, I knew I was going to have to describe the frightening health crises I went through in 2010, and though I have made a full recovery — for the most part — this wasn't something I fondly anticipated.

The ordeal began when my husband James and I were on our way back to our Atlanta home from a quick trip to Ann Arbor to visit friends. The time in Michigan, spent with Regina, one of my closest girlfriends from Spelman College, and her new husband (now former husband) had been full of lightness and laughter, a welcome respite from the stress of trying to keep Greening Youth Foundation growing into a viable nonprofit that could do good work and support our family at the same time. My sons were both attending an expensive private school, so the bills were more than a notion. I was putting in long nights and not getting enough sleep — anybody in business for herself knows exactly how that goes. It's essential that entrepreneurs learn how to carve out personal time, and search for the holy grail of work/life balance. At that point in 2010, just two years after I had started the nonprofit, needless to say I wasn't close to finding it yet — me and the holy grail weren't even in the same hemisphere. James was transitioning out of his law practice, and we both were working full-time for the foundation. Not to mention the fact that all of our savings had been sunk into the business. But I did enjoy the chance to get away, even if just for a few days, and bask in the comfort of an old friend.

After we landed back in Atlanta and got in the car at long-term parking to head home, we were still talking about how much fun the weekend had been. It would be only a matter of minutes before my mind would shift away from the weekend and back to my daily worries and anxieties. You know the drill: the joy of the moment falls away, and your mind inexorably pushes you back to the daily grind. We were riding along I-85 North, approaching downtown, laughing about something that had happened the night before. When I glanced over at James, he was looking at me with a strange expression on his face.

"Angelou?! What's wrong?" he asked.

I wasn't sure what he was referring to. I turned and looked at him fully. And I saw his concern quickly morph into extreme alarm. I don't remember anything after that. The next memory I had was opening my eyes in a hospital room and seeing the faces of my entire family peering down at me, all of them looking terrified, as if they had been spooked by a ghost.

James told me later on what happened in the car: When he looked over at me, the entire left side of my face was drooping, sliding downward as if tugged by gravity. He got on the phone immediately and called my mother, which was critical because the time on his cell phone was registered. Mom was also a nurse. She urged him to take the nearest exit and get me to a hospital. Luckily there was one less than a mile away, Atlanta Medical Center. At the hospital, his worst fears were confirmed: I was having a stroke. I was just 39 years old — still two months away from my 40th birthday — had been a vegetarian for nearly my entire life, regularly practiced yoga, never smoked, and exercised several times a week. In other words, the absolute last person anybody in their right mind would see as a stroke risk.

At the hospital, one of the doctors pulled James aside in the elevator. My husband couldn't help but notice that the doctor was actually excited, not the demeanor one might expect in the situation. He told James that I appeared to be an ideal candidate for a rare drug, called a clot buster, that could instantly reverse my fortunes. The doctor said there was a narrow group of people who could utilize this particular drug — nonsmokers below a certain age and weight — at the onset of a stroke. But he said there was a small possibility that the drug, essentially a high-powered blood thinner, could cause me to "bleed out" and die. He needed to know rather quickly what James wanted to do, because the drug needed to be administered soon after the stroke symptoms appeared. Needless to say, James was almost paralyzed with the heavy decision he had to make. He went out into the parking lot and called his own mother, tearfully telling her about the dilemma he faced. She coached him through his fears and hesitations. He knew that if I didn't get the drug and survived the stroke, I could be paralyzed for the rest of my life.

James walked back into the hospital and told the doctor that upon reflection he concluded that I would want him to go for it. So, they administered the drug. It worked; clearly, I did not perish. Three days later, I was back home with my very relieved but still shell-shocked family. It's no wonder why I now call my husband of 24 years my angel.

Once I made a full recovery, a pressing question quickly emerged: Why the hell did an exceedingly healthy 39-year-old woman suffer a stroke? I desperately needed some reasonable explanation, otherwise that six-letter word would forever hover over my head like a guillotine: stroke. Because what I discovered right away was that once you have one, you're much more likely than the average person to have another one. We will never know for sure exactly what brought about the stroke, but the doctors gave me some of their thoughts. One possibility was that there may have been some kind of connection to the birth control pills I was taking. But the most helpful analyses came from David, the psychotherapist I began to see to deal with my high level of anxiety after the ordeal. It was a form of post-traumatic stress disorder, this constant worry that I carried around everywhere I went: What if it happened again?

One day, David said to me, "You're teaching kids to be stewards of the environment, but you need to be your own steward." He told me

I hadn't been paying nearly enough attention to my health — mental and physical. He prescribed a medicine he said would have a dramatic effect on my well-being: He told me to walk outside. That was it. Every day, find at least 20 minutes to walk outside. What I heard was the word "walk," so I thought he was talking about exercise.

"Okay, I can just walk on the treadmill for 20 minutes," I said, already calculating in my head how I could fit that in.

But he was shaking his head. His emphasis was on the word "outside," not the word "walk."

"No, that's not enough. You have to be outside."

He said nature would be like a medicine of sorts — the healing powers of the green spaces would go to work on my psyche. I had been working in the environmental sphere for all these years, but it was the first time that someone told me I needed to follow my own counsel and find a way to get outside every day. Luckily we lived a block away from a park that had been carved out in a bustling, heavily trafficked Atlanta neighborhood around the Jimmy Carter Center. I obeyed my therapist, and I got out and started walking. I am so giddy to report, nearly a decade later, that it worked. Nature actually healed me. The anxiety I had bottled up inside slowly started to melt away. It rears its ugly head at times, but it has significantly dissipated. I began to feel more comfortable, to relax more. A big part of that was to let go of all the questions. I have a very logical personality — perhaps it's related to my law training, or perhaps I've always been this way. But I need rational answers: If you do A and B, then C will happen. But as I walked away my fears, I began to accept that life doesn't always work that way. Maybe there was no clear-cut explanation for why this thing happened to me. Maybe I just needed to let it go and learn how to live in the moment.

The memory of my outdoor healing came back to me in force recently when I learned of the theme for an upcoming conference called Shift, founded by environmentalist Christian Beckwith. The conference was focused on the connection between health and the outdoors. It's exciting to see the medical establishment diving so enthusiastically into this arena, now embracing what has been dubbed "eco-therapy." In 2017, Washington, DC-based physician Robert Zarr, one of the conference attendees, founded an organization called Park Rx America, which encourages more doctors to pull out their little pads and actually write park prescriptions for patients, particularly those with chronic diseases like hypertension and diabetes or with mental health challenges. Zarr, who writes an estimated 10 park prescriptions per day, according to a profile of him in *Time* magazine, says his prescriptions are only redeemable "outside, in the fresh air of a local park." In 2017, the *International Journal of Environmental Research and Public Health* analyzed 64 studies that focused on the effects of what they called "forest bathing" and found that the practice correlates to stress relief, less depression and anxiety, lower blood pressure, decreased heart rate, and more. In addition, many "eco-therapy" counselors actually conduct their sessions with patients outside to add outdoor healing to the session itself. Increasingly, people who work inside strapped to a computer are strongly being encouraged to get up from their desks every hour and, if they can't go outside, at least get to a window and look at greenery to be rejuvenated and more productive.

I talk throughout this book about the income divide that often keeps poor people from having access to green space. But you don't need the vastness of the Grand Tetons to get some of that healing. Your local park will do just fine. Of course, I know there's unfortunately a correlation between your income and how close your local park may be to where you live. That's one of the issues I was fighting to fix when I was out acquiring land for New Jersey and Georgia and the Trust for Public Land. So, I'm extremely sensitive to that disparity. But while we're working on those problems of access, I would implore all of us to do our best to give nature a chance to work its magic on us. I have to admit, when I first learned of nature's unique healing powers, I was stunned that there hasn't been more of an effort made to spread the word. Why was I just hearing about it at nearly age 40, having spent more than a decade immersed in the environmental world? I shook my head, once again remarking that Mother Nature desperately needs the services of one of those highly skilled marketing firms that can come in and do a dramatic transformation of the brand's image.

If Mother Nature had a makeover, the first group that the campaign would need to target is young people. In his ground-breaking bestseller, *Last Child in the Woods*, Richard Louv coined the term "nature-deficit disorder" over a decade ago to describe the disconnection that the current generation of young people have with nature, and how we all suffer mentally, physically, and emotionally when we fail to interact with nature on a regular basis. I have seen this dramatic change happen in my own life, with my children, so I feel his words acutely.

> The shift in our relationship to the natural world is startling, even in settings that one would assume are devoted to nature. Not that long ago, summer camp was a place where you camped, hiked in the woods, learned about plants and animals, or told firelight stories about ghosts or mountain lions. As likely as not today, "summer camp" is a weight-loss camp, or a computer camp. For a new generation, nature is more abstraction than reality. Increasingly, nature is something to watch, to consume, to wear—to ignore.
>
> Richard Louv, *Last Child in the Woods: Saving Our Children from Nature-Deficit Disorder*, Algonquin Books, 2005, p. 2

Just consider that Louv first introduced the concept of nature-deficit disorder in 2005, before cell phones took over the lives of nearly every breathing person on the planet, especially and most dramatically our children. I have spoken on many occasions about how my attraction to nature first occurred in the 1970s when I would travel with my family from the concrete and asphalt jungle of Jersey City to a small house my parents purchased in Upstate New York, in a town called Scio, not far from the Canadian border. Those carefree days running joyfully through vast verdant fields and playing for hours lost under the canopy of endless woods were transformative for me and my impressionable young mind. It took another two decades before I even realized exactly how transformative, when I left law school and found my way to the New Jersey Department of Agriculture. Working in land acquisition, driven by a desire to conserve lands for public use, I made the connection to my childhood, how all those hours and days outdoors embedded something deep in my soul that emerged years later, like a slow-blooming flower.

Even when I wasn't in Upstate New York playing in the woods, I still managed to spend most of my days outdoors in Jersey City — running up and down the streets, skipping, jumping Double Dutch, and playing jacks. We were burning calories, breathing in the air, giving nature a chance to keep us healthy and happy. (I should note that I lived two blocks away from the Holland Tunnel, with its endless traffic congestion fighting to get into Manhattan on the other side of the Hudson River, where the newly constructed Twin Towers stood tall — so I can't attest to the purity of the air we were breathing.) Up and out in the

Nick, Angelou, Helen (Mom), and Adrienne Chiles at tennis court in Upstate NY. CREDIT: WALTER CHILES

summer mornings, back inside after the sun had finally disappeared behind the looming overpass of the New Jersey Turnpike off in the distance. That was our lives, communing with the outdoors as often as we could. My appreciation of nature's beauty might have been even more developed than that of my peers on the block because of the particular interests of my beloved grandmother, Aline, who lived with us. She had a wicked green thumb and loved to surround herself with as many soaring, colorful flowers as could fit in the plot of dirt, maybe 3-foot by 6-foot, outside our brownstone. But her true masterpiece was the much larger green space in front of the church, Central Baptist, which sat two doors down from our house. Grandma was one of the church elders, and she had appointed herself as the queen of Central's gardens. Stretching across the front of the church for at least 50 feet was a 7-foot tall iron fence. Inside the fence, Grandma constructed her masterpiece — a lush, wondrous garden dense with the most colorful, durable flowers she could get her hands on, from sunflowers bursting with joy and attracting giddy swarms of bees to the marvel of Four O'clocks that somehow knew to display their beauty to the world every day at the same time. It all was a lovely sight to behold — an appropriate testament to the glory of the Lord, a sight relished by the church members on a Sunday afternoon as they flooded the church steps after service. I should note the reason why the flowers needed to be durable: my brother and his friends, during their daily wiffleball and stickball marathons, would invariably send a ball over the fence and into the garden. An entertaining game of cat-and-mouse would ensue as one of the boys — usually my brother was drafted for the task because he and his friends at least could assume that Grandma would be less likely to kill him — tried to wait Grandma out and choose a moment when she went inside or turned her head away to risk retrieving the ball. But she was the perfect sentinel because she rarely turned her head away from her beloved garden — and she was an avid baseball fan who enjoyed watching her grandson and his friends play ball. She could probably predict from the spin of the wiffleball and the trajectory of the line drive whether it was likely to land on top of a colorful

Grandma Aline, Angelou, and Mazi Chiles (Angelou's nephew) at Grandma's apartment in Jersey City. CREDIT: JAMES EZEILO

bed of her beloved Four O'clocks — and therefore some little black or Puerto Rican boy would have to die that day.

I would be conscripted to help Grandma dig down into the soil and plant the flowers, water them when needed, and generally fuss over their prosperity. Just like those hours upstate, this time not only latched me even more firmly to my grandmother's hip, but it also fixed me with a love for greenery that was lodged in my soul. My mother in these years was often busy running the family record store a couple of miles away or finishing her business degree at Rutger's University. So, it was me and Grandma, connecting over the flowers, the soil, the candies she would magically produce from the pockets of her colorful housecoats, the television shows we would watch together, the candy apples she would make so that I could have my first lessons in entrepreneurialism, the games she would watch me play with my friends. While the friends drifted away and my television tastes matured, I still have the flowers that will always sit next to my heart. (Right next to my jubilant obsession with the candy, which I still love far too much.)

When my sons were young, I was ecstatic that they would fill their days outside, exploring the critters in and around the small stream that ran through the front of our property in Georgia. I was pleased that they had fashioned their own version of my childhood, albeit far from the city streets where I grew up, staying outside for hours on end with their friends and their two female cousins, Mari and Lila, who are the same ages. If they weren't playing in the water and dirt, they were on the driveway basketball court or kicking a soccer ball back and forth. In fact, my mother perhaps got a bit too involved in one of their games when she fell onto the concrete driveway and broke her hip while rounding third in an impromptu game of baseball with her grandsons. But I must admit, if you're going to break your hip at age 70, trying to stretch a triple into a home run against your grandkids was probably the coolest way imaginable to do it.

My early joy at watching my boys grow up turned to concern when their hours outdoors grew shorter and shorter as they got older. The inescapable magnetism of video games began to take hold, just as they had seized control of the minds of every boy their age in America, as if some tech version of the zombie apocalypse took over our kids' brains. They still played sports, but now it was competitive organized sports, meaning too much of it was confined to scheduled practices at carefully organized times. The carefree spirit of play was slipping away. Because I was now immersed in the creation of the Greening Youth Foundation, I made sure that they got as much time outdoors as possible and had plenty of opportunity to appreciate the marvel of nature. But it was easy for me to understand how the phenomenon described by Louv in *Last Child in the Woods* had taken hold of the American childhood.

My boys even had their own battles with another phenomenon that's become too prevalent in our kids: asthma. Asthma has exploded in recent years and is now considered the most common chronic health disorder in children. My own boys grew out of it as they hit their middle-school years, which often happens with American children. Studies have shown that the brunt of the illness falls heaviest on blacks and Hispanics, measured by hospitalizations and asthma deaths. Black people are three times more likely to die from asthma than white people, as are Puerto Ricans, and three to six times more likely to visit the hospital. A big reason is that the indoor environmental allergens that can trigger asthma are much more common in places where blacks and Puerto Ricans live, such as dust mites, cockroaches, rodents, molds, and fungi. This points to inner-city life as the culprit; in studies that have controlled for inner-city residence, neither being black nor Hispanic nor in poverty were significantly correlated with the prevalence of asthma symptoms in childhood. Cockroaches are a particularly dastardly and acute trigger; not only are the little bastards disgusting, but they can cause illness as well.

Scientists have also studied the impact of the outdoors on asthma and found that pollution also can play a major role. Researchers from the University of Southern California discovered that in 10 Southern California cities, children living within 150 meters of a freeway were more likely to be diagnosed with asthma than children who lived further away. In addition, children who had higher levels of nitrogen dioxide, which is emitted by automobiles, in the air around their homes were more likely to develop asthma symptoms.

I discussed in the previous chapter how words like "organic" can have an exclusionary effect, but if we're going to talk about nature as healer, we have to look at how crucial food is to our health. I was delighted when I saw some of the young folks in Greening Youth discover for themselves in a dramatic way how much the kinds of food we eat can improve our health and well-being. Our Director of Programs, Eboni, enlisted her brother and his basketball teammates to participate in a teenage service project at GYF's Urban Conservation Training Institute in the historic West End of Atlanta. They did it very begrudgingly, showing up every day for a week to do various outdoor activities, like harvesting the crops and preparing other spaces for new crops. Every day they would eat the healthy food samples provided by our local farmer. To their surprise, they started noticing something: They had more energy. It got to the point where these big teenage basketball players started to change the way they wanted to eat. A few of them actually decided to become vegetarians; they started to spread their new discovery to their other teammates. They saw the big difference in the way they felt. I wanted to do backflips when I heard that story. When I talked to Eboni's brother recently, Khalil, I was ecstatic when he said he was still a vegan, two years after that fateful summer.

We had another group of teenagers in our Urban Youth Corps that would come in at the start of the summer with bags of Flamin' Hot Sweet Chili Cheetos and orange sodas. This was at 8 AM, before the work started. In other words, this was their breakfast. But our project manager at the time, Whitney, had different ideas. She's very health conscious, so she would start them off in the morning with fruits and nuts, salads, granola bars, and other healthy treats. After a while, they stopped bringing the Cheetos and soda and started looking forward to Whitney's food. Eventually they didn't want to eat the Cheetos at all; they began rejecting foods like that. It was a slow process, but we got them to the point where they could see the connection between how they felt later in the day and the food they ate. They were doing a full day of tough outdoor work that required endurance. When they were working with Cheetos on their stomachs, they would fizz out in the afternoon like their batteries had died; it really dragged them down. But with the better food, their energy was up and they could work a lot longer. It was so satisfying seeing the light go off without us having to bash them over the head. That's always the best way to teach teenagers.

But frankly, I'm always disturbed when we have to do these kinds of health-education campaigns with 17- and 18-year-olds; how have they gone this long and not heard any of this? Particularly teenage athletes who spend considerable time tending to their bodies. Why aren't high-school coaches making this a major priority? This gets me back to how badly Mother Nature needs a powerful marketing campaign to touch young people. If I were a high-school coach — and if you happen to be one reading this right now, listen up — I would be handing my team a list of foods that they should be eating at each meal. And I wouldn't stop there — I'd regularly quiz my players: "What'd you have for breakfast and lunch today?"

It's that important. Two of my nieces were serious softball players in high school. I was startled when I heard that one of their teammates — the pitcher, no less — passed out on the field in the middle of a game. When the girl's father ran onto the diamond to see about her, his first question to her when she stared up at him, wide-eyed, was, "When was the last time you ate?"

She had to think about it for a second. "Yesterday," she said.

I should add that it was about 7 PM when this occurred — and still well over 80 degrees. If I could, I'd add the bulging-eyes emoji right here.

We have failed to properly indoctrinate them with the message that the foods they put in their bodies have a direct link to how they feel and how they perform. I recently had an ongoing dialogue about this with one of the teenagers working on our urban youth corps, doing infrastructure work on a park in the West End of Atlanta. As I said, we own a 4.5-acre farm at Greening Youth's Urban Conservation Training Institute, and sometimes we feed the kids some of the fruit grown there. One morning, Derek looked contemptuously at all the fruit and granola bars we had available for breakfast.

"Why do I need to eat that for breakfast?" he asked. Loudly. Derek's disapproval was quite obvious.

I quickly saw it as a teaching opportunity. I asked him what he typically ate for breakfast. He answered, "Cheetos. Or whatever."

Derek likely knew Cheetos wasn't the world's healthiest breakfast, but he wanted me to make the case for the fruit and granola bars. I launched into an off-the-cuff soliloquy on the health benefits, how it would result in a big change in energy level, he wouldn't get tired as quickly, and it might even help his skin. From the look on his face, I could tell it was the first time he was hearing about these connections. It was mind-boggling to me that a 17-year-old had never heard this before. When I was done, he said something like, "Yeah, okay, we'll see."

In other words, he wasn't yet convinced. I was just some adult talking, blah, blah, blah, telling him things he didn't want to hear.

We have made nutrition a big part of our training program with young people. On a different occasion when I was telling them they should pack their own lunch because they probably wouldn't have time in the middle of the work day to stop and head to a fast-food restaurant, Derek was once again the voice of doubt.

"Yeah, but what if there's one really close?" he asked. "Then I'd have time to go."

"It's better for you to have an apple and a peanut butter and jelly sandwich and some water than McDonald's for lunch," I said.

My crusade with Derek is still a work in progress. But I return to the idea of the need for a marketing campaign for Mother Nature because I'm so disturbed that a 17-year-old could be so skeptical. If he hadn't been in our program, he clearly would have stepped into adulthood with a deficient picture of nutrition. And I can't help but wonder what has been going on in his home for the last 17 years: what was Derek seeing on his plate; what was he being told about the importance of healthy food? I know that there are so many more Dereks out there in the black community and elsewhere, kids who somehow have grown up without receiving basic information about such an important issue. What happened to the cartoons and commercials that taught me about the food groups and food pyramid when I was little, even if some of that information turned out to be somewhat questionable? At least we were being indoctrinated with the idea that our food was connected to our health. (Though I have to point out that such a message might be passed along in a public service announcement that would be followed by a commercial for Cap'n Crunch or Lucky Charms, cereals that were basically candy submerged in a bowl of milk.)

There's no doubt in my mind that one of our greatest enemies in trying to promote the healing effect of nature is the smartphone. In young people, in old people, in all people, these gadgets hypnotize us and keep us from basking in the wonder of the outdoors. But I'd like to point out that you can bring your phone with you when you go walking in the park. It might not be the ideal way to employ nature's healing powers, but it's better than sitting on the couch or behind the desk. Somehow, we need to learn how to merge these devices with nature.

When we introduce these technological innovations, unfortunately we can't gaze into a crystal ball to see how they might impact our health years down the line. If we did, we might make some different decisions in the early stages of a product's development. We could have designed phones that could only be used for a few hours a day or that had some kind of time limits for the apps. Or we could have promoted apps that forced you to go outside to use them. I was hopeful when Pokémon Go was the craze because it forced kids to get outside to locate and capture the Pokémon, but unfortunately that craze was very short-lived, at least among the kids in my circle. I'm just throwing out crazy examples, but the point is that we could have been more responsible in how we pushed these handheld computers to the masses, particularly our children. It was less than a decade ago when I remember parents being able to wait until their children were teens before they gave them a cell phone. Now such a notion would be laughable to a middle-schooler. I'm sure when Henry Ford was laboring on his prototypes for the gasoline-powered automobile at the start of the 20th century, he wasn't imagining that the mass production of his movable contraption would one day result in the suffocation of his planet with carbon dioxide.

One of the most disturbing new inventions I've come across with disastrous potential consequences is the use of carbon credits by wealthy individuals to offset their rapaciously eco-unfriendly lifestyles. Nations have been employing carbon credits for years now to give corporations the options of reducing their greenhouse gas emissions to meet predetermined limits or pay money to reduce emissions elsewhere. While there are many ethical questions to be raised by this approach, I understand how we've gotten to this point where the capitalist profit motive is the planet's most zealously treasured commandment. At least it takes us one big step in the right direction, which I can't take for granted in a political environment where we are still fighting to prove climate change is man-made. But personal carbon credits for individuals? We are now at a point where we are letting fabulously wealthy individuals reduce the guilt of their lifestyles by purchasing carbon credits to off-set the greenhouse gases being emitted by their extravagant lifestyle. If these rich folks are truly dedicated to saving the planet, is it too much to ask that they make changes in their lifestyles? Is it really too much of an imposition to live in a smaller house, or practice some kind of discipline in how much you use and emit, or to travel on a commercial aircraft instead of a private jet? Is that too unreasonable a request?

In this arena, it has never been clearer how the rules are made to benefit a tiny segment of the population. We conduct these widespread national campaigns to encourage the average person to recycle, reuse, and renew, to buy an electric car or hybrid, to be always mindful of their carbon footprints, but if you're rich, you can wave some cash around and buy back your right to be as rapacious as you want. This may sound ridiculous to some, but let's take that logic and apply it to other areas of our society, such as the criminal justice system. We have deemed that the dealers of illicit drugs are some of the most despicable characters who walk on Earth. But what if drug dealers were in the position to write their own rules and determined that it was okay that they sold illegal drugs to the masses, as long as they used a portion of their earnings to buy food and shelter for the needy? In other words, they could purchase an illegal drug credit, or offset. This would allow them to push their drugs without guilt, presuming that guilt is part of a drug dealer's emotional repertoire. Ironically, we have seen the equivalent of the illegal drug credit in many communities already, where drug dealers are hailed as community saviors because of the good they do in the community. Outsiders have decried the moral bankruptcy of such an arrangement, but I would contend that personal carbon credits aren't that radically different. In my mind, to be able to use your wealth to purchase carbon credits to offset the polluting that you are doing is such a farce. I guess that means we need to add to the services needed by Mother Nature: She also needs a lobbyist firm to work the halls of Congress. Of course, we already have organizations that would probably consider themselves the lobbyists for Mother Nature, but at this point, many of them are so tainted by politics that they are no longer very effective.

You might think this sounds like fantastical daydreaming, but I'm only half kidding. We have become so disconnected from Mother Nature that I think so often we lose sight of the gift she is to the world. Whether it's the power of the outdoors to heal our ailments or the goodness of the food she produces, we have somehow gotten far away from understanding who she is and how the Creator has presented us with this magical entity so attuned to the needs of the human body. It's no accident that our chronic diseases, our mental state, our physical instrument are all precisely calibrated to respond to nature in the most positive ways. We are animals, created to live amid the natural environment and derive everything we need from it. It is tragic to me how thoroughly we seem to have forgotten this.

CHAPTER 4

Activating a New Generation

W**HEN I WAS A LITTLE GIRL,** I would sit in wonder and watch my grandmother carefully cut up peaches, apples, and other fruit and preserve it in Mason jars that she stored in the basement of our family's brownstone in Jersey City. Sometimes she'd even let me help her prepare the preserves and then take them downstairs and carefully place them on wooden shelves. It wasn't until decades later that I even encountered words like "permaculture" and even longer before I connected some of these modern concepts with what my grandmother was doing in the basement 40 years ago. Back then there wasn't a fancy word connected to it. But it brought home to me quite forcefully the thought that people of color have been connecting in a direct way to the environment for a very long time — despite the thinking these days that such a connection is a "white" thing.

When I was a child in the 1970s, the first time I ever thought about the responsibility of humans to protect the Earth actually came by way of a commercial that ran frequently in the New York tri-state area. It featured a Native American man dressed in full regalia, so that viewers would quickly look at him and think "Indian." First, he rowed his canoe on a body of water that was littered with food wrappers and garbage. The camera panned out, and we saw that there were ships and factories belching smoke nearby. He stepped out of the canoe to find garbage on the shore. Then he stood by the side of the road and watched someone throw trash out of a moving car. A tear rolled down his cheek, letting us know that all the trash made him sad. "People start pollution. People can stop it," the voice-over said, as the logo for the "Keep America Beautiful" campaign showed on the screen.

That was the first image I had of someone being upset about the mistreatment of the environment. The creators of the campaign decided to go all the way back and use the original natives of this land to make the case for Mother Nature. Whatever happened to that idea? Somehow, a narrative that started with the original Americans got changed over the ensuing decades to the stereotype that people of color aren't connected to the land. (Never mind the revelation years later that the actor playing the Native American chief was actually of Italian American descent.)

One of the reasons I started GYF was I sensed that if we had any chance of stopping the full-throttled mess we're making of our environment, the momentum needed to come from young people. But as we discovered when we first went into that all-black elementary school in Atlanta, one of the biggest obstacles among youth of color was fighting the image they have implanted in their brains from an early age of who is an environmentalist. This is an exercise that would work with just about anybody who has spent more than five minutes in America: If I ask you to take a minute to conjure an image of an outdoorsman, an environmentalist, who do you see in your mind's eye? I would guess most of you come up with a rugged-looking white guy, probably with a beard, wearing flannel, khaki or camo colors, and serious hiking boots. Where did that image come from, and how do we change it, broaden it, supplement it, so that young kids of color (male and female) can imagine their own faces supplanted over that white guy's? In many ways, that is the primary question addressed in this book and one of the main driving forces behind the Greening Youth Foundation.

In an earlier chapter, I referenced the quote from the late astronaut/teacher Sally Ride: "You gotta see it to be it." What we are trying to do inside the movement we have started at GYF is to get our kids to see it, to understand what is possible for them. Slowly but surely, we are changing their perception of who can work in environmental professions, who visits national parks and forests, who vacations or goes camping in the outdoors, who recycles and composts, who cares. One of the earliest ways we endeavored to spark the imagination of young people was with our Green Speakers Series. This was essentially a Career Day for the environment, where we brought in a variety of professionals (the majority were diverse) engaged in environmental work to get these young folks to start envisioning themselves pursuing such careers. As I said in chapter 1, one of the most effective speakers was Ovie Mughelli, who at the time was an All-Pro fullback for the Atlanta Falcons. I heard through a colleague in the environmental community that Ovie had an interest in the issue, so we reached out to him. When he arrived at the first school, I got a chance to see up close how much of a difference celebrity makes, particularly with young people. We had been talking to these kids in our EcoForce clubs about a wide variety of environmental issues that we were trying to get them interested in, with varying degrees of success. But when this athlete strode into the room, wearing his Atlanta Falcons jersey, looking like a superhero, they were instantly enthralled. They hung on his every word as he encouraged them to do more, to become true environmental stewards. The energy in the room was incredible. We had tried mightily to make all the materials as interesting as we could, in most cases starting from scratch because there just wasn't a lot of existing resources we could use to talk about these issues with children. Not many educators had tried to create a curriculum to make discussion of renewables and composting fun for elementary and middle-school students of color, so we were mostly on our own. If we were going to keep them engaged, much of it would depend on the delivery. We created games to get them hooked, like a recycle relay and an obstacle course, almost tricking them into absorbing the material. But the celebrity factor did much of the work for us.

After Ovie, we brought in different eco-entrepreneurs to talk about the companies they had started, in areas like waste management, recycling, solar panels. They weren't celebrities, but I felt like we were making some headway in changing the students' perception of what an environmentalist looks like. We hadn't yet connected with the federal government, so the national park rangers and other workers weren't yet on our radar. Increasingly, however, what was creeping onto my radar were jobs. Because when we moved up and started working with high-school students, I saw a vast number of black and Hispanic kids who couldn't find jobs. This was right after the financial crisis of 2009, so the job market was still in a tenuous state, especially for young people of color. (It seems like it *always* is for them.) At the same time, as I began to learn more about the business side of the environmental world, I saw there was an enormous need for more workers, in practically every sector of the industry. For me, it was a no-brainer: Why don't we bring these two needs together into one lovely solution?

I will talk about environmental careers in more detail in the next chapter, but there is clearly a link between pulling more young people into these careers and activating the next generation to become fighters on behalf of the environment — basically, to become activists. I see it every day, when I watch young people go from disinterested teens merely looking for a summer job to engaged, knowledgeable, and often outraged observers of our national environmental emergency. I see them become activated, like a switch has been flipped. It's similar to the activation you often see when a young person lands on a college campus and suddenly becomes the world's angriest militant. They begin to see the atrocities everywhere they look and understand that it is their generation and that of their children that will bear the brunt of the horrendous decisions that older generations continue to make. We are mortgaging their futures for our own selfish needs, effectively snatching up their inheritance like it is a wad of cash and taking it on an extended and ridiculous spending spree. They see this, and they are not happy about it at all. A Kenyan proverb that is engraved on a bracelet that I often wear states, "The earth was not inherited from your parents but was borrowed from your children." That says it all. This proverb is also profound to me as my absolute shero is Kenyan — Dr. Wangari Maathai, the first African woman to win the Nobel Peace Prize for her work in sustainable agriculture and environmental activism.

When you talk about creating environmental stewards, it's not necessary for that young person to become a tree-care expert or a park ranger or a wildlife biologist to have an enormous effect. They don't even have to go into a career connected to the environment. The most crucial thing is to open their eyes, to permanently alter the lens through which they look at the world. From that moment forward, almost like by osmosis, everything they do will be done with an eye toward sustainability. They won't be able to help themselves; they'd be mortified to discover that their activities were harming the planet. If they go into the entertainment industry, they will have the protection of the Earth's resources in the back of their mind as they scout locations for a movie shoot or dispose of waste from craft services. The architects will have solar energy and massively reducing a building's energy footprint at top of mind. Doctors will look around and start advocating for a more environmentally friendly way of disposing of medical waste. Whatever their field, they will be sure to make a difference. We need people with this Earth-friendly mentality in every sector of the economy, making their presence felt. It might take a decade or two before we start seeing the results of our current work, but I'm certain they will make an impact.

There is also a subtle racial shift that begins to happen among white people when we bring kids of color into this environmental world. White children will grow up watching African Americans, Native Americans, or Latinos doing this work, and it will permanently transform their idea of who is an environmentalist. My hope is that if I walk into a classroom in 20 years and ask any group of kids, no matter their color or background, what an environmentalist looks like, not only will they be able to break down in stunning detail what an environmentalist is but they will have a picture in their head of what one looks like that reflects diversity. And all of them, black or white or Latinx or Native or Asian, will be teaching their own kids about alternative energy and renewable energy. They will be composting their own garbage and living in a house whose footprint is infinitesimal. That is my testimony, my prayer.

We hold a fun annual event to get our young people used to the idea of living in the outdoors, the Legacy Campout. We bring nearly

100 young people into the Martin Luther King Jr. National Historical Park in Atlanta, which is run by the National Park Service, to pitch tents and camp out under the stars — albeit a stone's throw from the looming Atlanta skyline and Interstate 85. We're trying to get them to see that, even in the heart of urban America, they are still surrounded by the outdoors. They quickly realize that camping out is something that is done by black kids from the city, not just white people on TV. After pitching their tents, they are treated to a variety of activities: dance performances, movies, storytelling. Of course, we always make s'mores. One year, Sally Jewell visited the campout when she was Secretary of the Interior during the Obama administration. It's one of my favorite GYF events every year — though I must admit that I have been known to slip out and get some shut-eye in my own bed at some point during the night; those kids wear me out! Superintendent Judy Forte is always there till the very end. This event is a prime example of activating the next generation, getting right to the heart of GYF's core mission.

The young people are gently eased into the act of camping out, in a less intimidating way that is more likely to yield a positive experience. We're also much more likely to get a thumbs-up from parents and caregivers than if we brought them deep into the woods right away. I remember one time the GYF staff went a little too far with trying to recreate a bona fide camping experience for the students. It is really funny now when I think about it, but at the time it wasn't funny at all. (Okay, I think it was actually my idea.) We wanted the students to experience one of the scariest things about camping in the outdoors — the bears! So, after telling ghost stories and getting the kids successfully scared (in good fun), we then used a flashlight to create a bear shadow on their tents, sending some of the older teenagers running and screaming. What a blast! They took it in stride and later agreed that it was quite hilarious. Admittedly, we chose the teenagers because they were too cool to participate in most of the storytelling and we could tell they thought it was *corny*. Well, needless to say, we had their full attention for the rest of that night. We were all surprised to see that those same students came back the next year.

Angelou Ezeilo, Audrey Peterman, and Superintendent Judy Forte at Legacy Campout. CREDIT: YERO WINBORNE

I can agree that camping out can be kind of scary the first time you do it. Even when my family was visiting our house in Upstate New York every year, we spent our evenings inside the house. On a few terrifying occasions, something from the outside made its way to the inside. There were lots of bats one night, accompanied by plenty of screaming from the kids. I think my mom might have screamed a couple of times, too. Another time there was a big snake. My dad got rid of the critters each time, but we were reminded that we were just visitors in their space. But outside at night we did not go. There was no sleeping in a tent for us in the 1970s — perhaps connected to the fact that we were the only black family for miles around. My parents would rather be behind a door that locked. But this never deterred my adoration for our summer home upstate, which we all referred to as "up in the country."

In fact, I was about 10 the first time I actually camped out, as a Girl Scout in New Jersey. I had just graduated from being a Brownie and was now a Junior, super excited about our impending camping trip at Eagle Island. There was a big group of us going. We all were thrilled because there wasn't a lot of camping that happened in Jersey City. I remember being really anxious for many reasons though. You see, we were going to an island. We were going to swim and camp. On the outside, I couldn't contain my excitement. But, in retrospect, I was quite scared to swim and to camp — neither activity was done often among my group of friends. This could explain why I am not the strongest swimmer to this day. I know not being a strong swimmer is kinda cliché for a brown city girl. This is why I made a conscious effort to enroll in every Mommy and Me swimming class I could find when I had my two sons. I am happy to report that my boys are both human fish; in fact, one is even a certified lifeguard.

Back to the camping trip; when we got to the venue it seemed really dark and creepy since we arrived at night. This didn't help my fear that was steadily mounting. I'm not sure what I was expecting. I had read that there would be no bathrooms — and I already had to go so bad. And I knew we would not be taking a shower until we returned home. I knew that we would be sleeping in tents, but I also heard there were creatures that came out at night. Bottom line: I didn't know what was going to happen to me, but I was quite sure it would result in me crying and wanting to go home.

I was happily surprised and relieved the next day when the campout amounted to us sitting around a bonfire making what I later learned to be s'mores and telling ghost stories. I wasn't too fond of the ghost stories, but being in the open air at night with my friends, eating s'mores and being scared together, is one of my favorite childhood memories. After my first camping experience, I couldn't get enough. I was always first to sign up when the opportunity presented itself again.

We see evidence every day of the mushroom effect of our work. When we do environmental-related education with elementary school students, their family members tell us how it begins to change family dynamics, family behaviors. Their older siblings then take the messages to their peers, and the teenagers in that family's sphere begin to have conversations they never had before about protecting the Earth.

When we bring high-school and college students into our internship programs, we see the changes even more dramatically. If they spend part of a summer in a national park and start to have their eyes opened to the beauty and glory of the outdoors, they want their family members to share their joy. "Why don't you come out and visit me here?" they will say to their mother or father or aunt one day. We are constantly having interns send us pictures they've taken next to a smiling parent surrounded by some incredible vista, in a part of the country that the parent has never visited. I get so excited when I see these because it's such a clear-cut illustration of the message and mission of GYF. As soon as she gets back home, that parent is heading straight to church and telling everybody who will listen about how wonderful the trip was and how proud she is of her child. Next thing you know, the entire church is planning a massive trip, to outdoor wonders like the Grand Canyon and also powerful historical sites like the Martin Luther King Jr. National Historical Park in Atlanta or the Charles Young Monument in Ohio, celebrating one of the original buffalo soldiers, or the Brown v. Board of Education National Historic Site in Topeka, Kansas. We see it happening all the time. Typically, these sites have not made it onto the radar of most African American families, much to the chagrin of the National Park Service. But that is starting to change; I'd like to think we're having something to do with that. I think many people would be surprised to discover how many fascinating sites central to African American history are being preserved by the National Park Service: places like Booker T. Washington's home, Bethune Cookman's home, George Washington Carver's home. If you've ever wondered what kinds of jobs a history major might snag when she graduates from college, well, an interpreter at one of these historical sites is a good answer.

Once a young person's eyes have been opened, they become a different person; they will never go back to their previous state of indifference. They become explorers, outdoorsmen and outdoorswomen, adventurous spirits. Little by little, we start chipping away at that image of the white guy with the beard, standing astride a mountain, gazing into the fabulous vista. Interestingly, we actually got approached by a branding company that wanted to work with us on a logo for GYF that would put this revamped image of an outdoorsmen into a logo. They had scoured our website and thought that we needed to do stronger brand-ing on what this new environmentalist looked like. They had seen the vast array of pictures on our Instagram account and were struck by how startling and progressive the images were, of young people of color doing things we were not accustomed to them doing. We heard them loudly and clearly. We are in the process of revamping our social media images so that it beautifully reflects our audience and the people we serve.

When you step into this environmental space and look around, you might be blown away by the things that are going on outside of the public's eye. Rue Mapp's fabulous nonprofit, Outdoor Afro (you can find more info in appendix 1), had an all-black crew that journeyed to the summit of Mount Kilimanjaro — not something most of us associate with black people. Examples like this are everywhere of a new generation of people of color diving into outdoor exploration and activism. There are events like Color the Crag Climbing Festival that celebrates diversity in the sport of rock climbing and organizations — including Brothers of Climbing, Brown Girls Climb, and National Association of Black Scuba Divers — with an astounding array of missions so mind-blowingly cool that they would bring a smile to your face.

Now when I'm at an environmental conference and hear someone bemoaning their inability to find any black or brown people who are interested in the issues, I immediately call *bullshit*. They're out there. When I open a catalogue from outdoor manufacturers and I get all the way to the last page without seeing a black or brown person climbing a mountain to show off their new boots, I call *bullshit*. If I see such tone-deafness, I have to conclude that company actually worked *not* to include people of color. I have a hard time hearing their excuses. My immediate reaction is I thought you wanted to make money, increase profits? Why wouldn't you try to expand your customer base? I have gotten incredibly exasperated by the same experience, over and over: I walk out my front door for yet another conference, leaving my family behind, rushing to the airport, boarding yet another flight, making my way to the venue with a big exhale of relief. When I grab the requisite glass of cabernet at the opening reception and look around the space, once again either I am the only black woman in the room, or our numbers are so miniscule we could hold our own conference in a phone booth (if we still had phone booths). I don't even need to single out any particular culprit here; rest assured that the scene is repeated at almost any one of them related to the environment or the outdoor-retailer industry. The paltry numbers continue to astonish me. Surely this is reflecting a certain indifference — I shouldn't be surprised when I open up the catalogues and see nothing but an unending parade of white faces.

I'd like for the environmental sector to think about this issue with the future in mind. Wouldn't we be so much more powerful a force if our team of fighters looked more like America? Even if there's not a pressing desire inside the environmental bubble to be as inclusive as possible, we need to just think about it more like an army engaged in a battle for our very survival. Take a page out of the actual US Army, which long ago recognized that it needed to expand its arms as wide as possible to be all it could be. Now it is one of the most diverse large organizations in the world. After recent federal efforts to dismantle decades of exhausting work to protect the Earth, we need as many allies as we can find. We have to be much more strategic and creative about how we conduct ourselves. If the environmental movement continues to be seen by most Americans of all colors and classes as a cute hobby for wealthy white elites, we will have done the planet a huge disservice. I have been heartened to see young people engaging in the fight, with organizations like Sunrise demonstrably showing how much young people passionately care about the issue. But even that group feels too white, too much like the white children of the white elite. I welcome their engagement, but I want more. I would implore any groups of young environmental activists in the same way I implore their parents: reach out and embrace as many allies as you possibly can.

When I reflect on that commercial I saw when I was a child, of the Native American shedding a tear when he observed the heedless ignorance of the littering Americans, I can't help but to ask myself what happened: How did we get so far away in the ensuing decades from that image of Indigenous peoples as the true stewards of the Earth? How did the teary-eyed chief morph into the wealthy white family shopping at REI? I would venture a guess that when most Americans think of Native Americans now, their thoughts are more likely to wander to casinos and, unfortunately, maybe even poverty and alcoholism. No longer are they seen as the original environmentalists. But how might the condition of the planet be different if the last few decades had gone in another direction: if we had decided as a community to lift up farmers (black, white, and Latinx), migrant workers, scientists, botanists, even hunters as the true symbols of environmentalism — people whose life's work, whose livelihood, whose passion is directly connected to the condition of the planet. It would have been beautiful if things had evolved this way. I shake my head at the missed opportunity. It's stunning to think that hunters likely see environmentalists as the enemy, even as we toil to protect the habitats of the animals they hunt. Yes, of course, many environmentalists would balk at the idea of killing any living creature, for sport, for food, for anything. But there are certainly hunters within our movement, too. We should be a diverse and nuanced bunch. Our tent should be big enough to include everybody, but yet it feels like it actually has become narrower.

The opposition forces have been able to keep us divided into separate camps. The conservatives will say they're the ones that want you to have a job and be able to put food on your table while the environmentalists care more about polar bears and the black-footed ferret than you and your future. So they implore people to fight against us if they wish to have a real shot at a solid quality of life. It's a ridiculous divide with a specious logic, but unfortunately it's been wildly successful. With its blind adherence to homogeneity, the environmental movement has not been agile and forward-thinking enough to combat it.

The point I'm making here is that the movement is damaged every day that its most prominent spokesman in the public's eye is a wealthy white man. This may seem like an obvious point, yet it still seems to escape too many powerful and influential figures inside the circles where I spend a lot of my time. If I'm at a conference and the voices participating in the discussion are missing an enormous swath of the American public, then that discussion is necessarily going to be too stunted and limited to be as effective as it could be. There are going to be enormous blind spots.

But it's not too late. I guess that's the message, too, because it's going to have to happen eventually; that is, if we're going to save this planet. Pivotal connections are being made with diverse groups of people of color, though we need many more. If you check the results of bond referenda on environmental issues, you will find that people of color are even more protective of the environment than white people — we instinctively understand that the survival of the planet is so much more crucial than some corporation's revenue. And frankly, we are still watching in astonished disbelief when we see so many white people in the US who don't seem to get that. If white liberals don't start making moves to embrace groups of color, they are going to become increasingly irrelevant, bulldozed by the more powerful forces that are motivated by greed and self-interest.

My goal is to work so hard that I put myself out of business, to look up one day and realize that GYF is no longer necessary. How will I know when society has reached that point? There's a little black girl who hasn't been born yet — not yet even a twinkle in her mom's and dad's eye. But she will be born one day in the future, emerging into a crazy, complicated world that seems unable to solve the problems of its own creation. That little girl will decide that she is surrounded by wonder and beauty that needs to be protected, preserved, cherished. And she will make an instantaneous decision that it is her job to be the Earth's protector. Her decision will feel organic, comfortable, well within her reach. Why? Because the society she is a part of will have sent her the message that the environment is something that belongs to everyone and that everyone bears an equal responsibility for protecting and preserving it. She will look in catalogues for outdoor retailers and see herself reflected in the pages. She will look at television commercials for vacationing at the Grand Canyon and see her family represented. She will look at Congress and see women who look like her mother and her auntie giving speeches from the floor of the Senate. This little girl will be no more likely to look for permission from white liberals to be enjoined in an environmental movement than she would ask them what she should eat for dinner. From the first day she emerges, she will be empowered. When that day comes, I can retire to my rocking chair — a nice glass of Malbec at my side, Stevie Wonder playing softly, a great book on my lap — and bask in the wonder of the glorious sunset.

CHAPTER 5

Careers

B ASED ON MY MANY YEARS of experience in the workforce, I knew that the presence of African American employees can make a big difference in the culture and decision-making of a workplace in unexpected ways. But I got a jolt when one of our young people presented that lesson on a silver platter to high-ranking federal officials at a ceremony in Washington, DC.

It occurred at the culminating event for one of our flagship programs with the National Park Service, the Historically Black College and University Internship (HBCUI) program, in which we work with the National Park Service, a component of the Department of the Interior. HBCUI places about four dozen students from historically black colleges and universities in NPS sites across the country, ranging from Yosemite and the Grand Canyon to the Little Rock Central National Historic Site and the Booker T. Washington birth home. What I love about these internships is that they educate about the indelible contributions African Americans have made to this nation, and they reveal to students the breadth of opportunities available to them in the natural resource management field. In fact, I find myself often talking to students about the range of disciplines that are needed in these federal land management agencies. It doesn't begin and end at park ranger. I was floored when I was first exposed to all the talents the park service is seeking to operate its 418 properties, including 60 parks — everything from lawyers to accountants, architects, historians, to musicians.

Yes, even musicians. We recruit our students based on the needs expressed by a particular site. For instance, there is a national park in New Orleans focused on jazz. We talked to a student from Hampton University who was a jazz pianist.

"Surely there couldn't be a job for me within the park service," he said to our Project Manager during a recruitment event.

Well, that summer he was playing piano at the New Orleans Jazz National Historic Park, located in the Tremé neighborhood near the French Quarter.

At the DC event, one of our interns, Shenise Cason, was recounting to Sally Jewell, the Secretary of the Interior at the time, the highlight of her summer. Rock Creek Park, which bisects the northwest quadrant of Washington, DC, was created by an Act of Congress in 1890, and today is administered by the National Park Service. Shenise had been on the interpretive team at Rock Creek Park working on an astronomy project called Night Skies in Africa. It was an exciting assignment for Shenise, a zoology major. But as she told us that day in Washington, she noticed something when she showed the elementary school students the film: after seeing the film, they were saddened and melancholy. It was puzzling to Shenise because she knew this piece was created especially for elementary-aged children. After watching the same reaction over and over, she realized that the problem was where the film opened. Because it was about the Night Skies in Africa, the film opened up talking about slavery and focused on the brutalities enslaved Africans endured in America. Shenise realized that the history needed to begin before American slavery; it needed to go back further and talk about the lives of these enslaved Africans and their ancestors on the African continent. She asked for permission from her superiors to work on a new script that would be presented to students. When she got a thumbs-up, she wrote an entirely new presentation that started with many of the glorious African kingdoms that predated European colonialization. She also was sure to end the film with the election of Barack Obama. When her superiors read it, a light bulb went on — they realized that Shenise was correct, the history needed to be seriously revamped.

As I heard Shenise present her story, I wondered to myself what was the likelihood that someone other than an African American young lady would have picked up on the sadness of the little ones and decide to do something about it? It was a wonderful moment for me because it brought home the essential need for an organization like GYF and how much of a difference we could make in many lives.

We had been doing our environmental education work in schools, running our EcoForce after-school clubs, when we heard about an RFP from the Department of the Interior that was offering a $2 million grant to develop programs to work with young people at NPS sites. We pulled together our collective brains and responded to the RFP with a proposal that we thought was pretty good. One day we got a call from George McDonald, the Director of Youth Programs for NPS, who had seen our proposal and was reaching out to chat with us. He was thrilled to learn of our existence because he had never run across an African American organization doing the work we were doing. A Hampton graduate himself, he told us how his older brother, Moriba, had brought him into the park service. He said the work was quite fulfilling, but most people of color were not aware that his world existed. In us, he saw an opportunity to start changing that.

But as we started to learn more about how the grant was structured, we realized that it wasn't as straightforward as we had thought. It wasn't like NPS was going to hand us a check for $2 million and tell us to get to work. No, it wasn't actually a traditional grant — it was more like an "opportunity" to get funding, where we would be reimbursed by NPS for work we did. We had a meeting with a few NPS administrators like Priscilla Nalls (RIP), who gave us more details. But James and I, both skeptical attorneys, walked away even more unsure about the soundness of the venture. They were basically telling us we would have to approach individual NPS sites and convince them to use GYF to do particular projects, then NPS would reimburse us after the projects were done. And not only that, but the NPS would only provide 75 percent of the funding, and we would have to provide 25 percent. We were dumbfounded.

"Wait, what?" we said. "Why would we ever do that?"

Judy Forte, who was superintendent of the Martin Luther King National Historic Park, brought us out to lunch after the meeting, along with Audrey Peterman, an influential environmental consultant and author. Both have since become dear friends of mine. I will always be grateful for the guidance they offered me and James that day. Forte, to her credit, started out by saying, "I know that this sounds really crazy...."

They told us that we didn't have to match the NPS money with our own funds; it could be in-kind resources rather than cash. Forte said an organization like ours was so desperately needed in the field because the large organization that at the time was dominating youth corps work was extremely homogeneous and was not reaching diverse students. They told us that we were well-positioned because we were both lawyers, meaning we would be better able than most new non-profits to negotiate the complicated minutiae of federal contracts and understand the budget circulars. Forte said we could start out with projects through the Martin Luther King Jr. National Historical Park in Atlanta, and Peterman promised to put us in touch with Alan Scott, her close colleague who worked at the Everglades National Park. They both assured us that, once we established a solid reputation, other parks would follow.

After we decided to take the plunge, our timing proved to be spectacular on a couple of different fronts. The first bit of good fortune came as a result of the catastrophic financial crisis that engulfed the country in 2008 and 2009. We came along on the heels of that, just as the federal government was throwing a chunk of stimulus money at federal agencies to provide jobs. Our first big project was actually in the Intermountain Region of the park service — we were tasked with connecting at-risk young adults (we no longer use this term because of its negative connotations; "at-promise" is now preferred) from the Denver area to 10 park sites in the intermountain region, where they would first complete an audit of the sites then prepare an assessment to determine their energy consumption in an effort to reduce their carbon footprints.

Our VP of Operations, Mike Fynn, a Georgia Tech-trained, LEED-certified engineer, brought these young people to the sites, including the Grand Canyon, and they conducted assessments of the visitors' centers to figure out their energy consumption. Even though many of the young people lived in the same area as the sites, it was the first time that most of them had ever been on the premises — and they were blown away. They were Native American, African American, Latinx American, some were homeless, all of them had had challenges. The group included a few women, but it comprised mostly young men who hadn't had many strong male figures in their lives; they saw Mike as a mentor. In fact, he's still in touch with some of them a decade later. We got Toyota to come on board as a sponsor, so Mike got in Prius vehicles with them and they hit the road. This project went on for almost two years. We called it the Green Project, took lots of pictures, chronicled it on social media sites that were just starting out. It was wildly successful, proving how much of a help we could be to NPS sites. After the Green Project, we started a big project with the Florida Everglades and another one with the MLK Historic Site. We were on our way, starting to get the groove of how to structure these programs. We learned that the best method for us was to recruit young people from the area around the project, and they would quickly fall in love with the site and the work.

As Forte had predicted, we began to develop a reputation as an organization that worked magic with a population that NPS had never engaged before. Soon other agencies began reaching out to us, such as the US Forest Service, which is in the Department of Agriculture — as opposed to the Department of the Interior where most of the federal land management agencies reside — and which oversees more than 150 national forests and nearly two dozen national grasslands. Upon further investigation, we discovered why federal agencies began stepping out of the shadows to seek our services. This was our second bit of fortuitous timing — the new Obama administration had begun to look more closely at the federal agencies and rate them on the diversity of their workforces, on how much they looked like the country they

served. Most of them, like Agriculture and Interior, were getting fail-
ing ratings, and they were suddenly desperate to find some diversity.
During this time, I was even invited to the White House to witness the
signing of the Presidential Memorandum, America's Great Outdoors
(AGO). My friend Rue Mapp of Outdoor Afro and I had to scrape
pennies together to attend the event. Rue and I conspired and crashed
in a hotel room together; there was no way we were going to miss
this day, which was so relevant to our work — no matter how broke
we were. I was sitting a couple of rows away from the stage with Rue.
Audrey Peterman was in the room, as well as Senator Cory Booker,
a longtime friend of the family. The AGO memorandum called for
support from private industry, local communities, Native American
leaders, and volunteers to protect natural places, monuments, and
features in the American landscape for future generations to come.
Amongst many other features of this memorandum was a call for
federal land management agencies to engage communities that represented the diverse tapestry of society. Well, this is what GYF was all
about. The AGO memo put GYF's mission in high gear, of engaging
underrepresented youth and young adults while connecting them to
the outdoors and careers in conservation.

Since I mentioned how broke I was, I feel like I need to point out,
especially for the budding entrepreneurs who might be reading this,
how much of our savings James and I used in the establishment of
GYF. Unlike Ruth and Mike, who had spouses with well-paying jobs,
James and I jumped in without a parachute. I remember us walking
around with our paychecks in our backpacks for weeks because there
wasn't enough money in the account for us to cash our checks. I am
proud to say that we never missed a payroll for our students — they
always got paid.

Once we got wind of this new direction from the administration,
we knew it was a great opportunity for us. Worried about our ability to quickly scale up, we even approached the Student Conservation
Association (SCA) and offered to be their diversity arm — they
could rely on us to recruit young people of color for their internship

programs. But SCA shut that down pretty quick; they had little interest in what we were offering.

The Forest Service (FS) wanted us to work with high-school students, which strongly appealed to us. I must commend the Forest Service for their creativity over the years; they have actually topped NPS as our biggest client. They love what we do, and they trust us to deliver. They now come to us and say, "We have money, we trust you guys, what do you think? Can you put together a program?" At one point, Michelle Mitchell, one of our key champions and a thought leader at FS, told us, "We're just going to start throwing stuff at you guys, and you just let us know when it gets to be too much." In other words, say uncle when we couldn't handle it anymore. We haven't said uncle yet. In the most recent fiscal year, our business with the Forest Service exceeded $2 million, just above the park service numbers.

We've also started with other agencies, such as the Bureau of Land Management, National Oceanic and Atmospheric Administration, and the Bureau of Reclamations. I believe one of the major reasons we have become so popular is that every one of these agencies is staring at a catastrophe looming on the horizon — the aging of their workforce, which some are calling the Silver Tsunami. I recently saw internal data provided by one of our project managers in DC that said as much as 75 percent of the NPS workforce is about to retire. They don't have a replacement plan; they don't have a pipeline of new hires — of any color. They all are deathly afraid that one of these days Americans are going to arrive at the Great Smokies, bursting with anticipation, and find the park closed down because NPS doesn't have enough employees to manage the park. It's easy to see why GYF has become the prettiest girl at the prom.

The last time I checked, our numbers revealed that 11 percent of our interns have gone on to take full-time jobs within these federal agencies, turning this work into a career. In fact, our interns are in such high demand that we have now turned into the decision-making authority for our national internship programs, requiring the individual sites to submit proposals to us and we decide which ones will get

GYF interns. We have created a template, with questions for the sites to answer in their proposals. These are some of the issues their proposals must address:

- Have you created a mentorship program for your intern?
- Is there a development program for your intern?
- How have you dealt with diversity in the past?
- What types of community resources are there surrounding your park?

They know that when they come to us, they must have strong answers to these questions to have any chance to be chosen. We bring together a panel of 5 or 6 judges to review the proposals and grade them on a scale of 1 through 5. In recent years, we've been getting up to 80 proposals from sites to employ our interns, so we have to pick in the range of 30 or 40 winners with each round. When judging the proposals, we also look at such questions as whether the site is too remote to send our young people. We're not comfortable relegating a 19- or 20-year-old to someplace that's going to feel like Siberia to them, otherwise they will have a negative experience. These fears led us to employ a buddy system. If a park or forest is in a town that's extremely remote, we will insist that at least two GYF interns work at the site together. This gives the students comfort and reassures the parents that their baby is not out in this unfamiliar terrain alone.

I have to chuckle when I think about the reactions our young people have been getting at these sites. Parks are so impressed with them that they don't want to let them leave — and don't seem to really believe us when we assure them that there are thousands of others behind them who are just as good. We had one young lady named Blue from Miami who made such a strong impression that the park kept extending her internship, finding new projects for her to do. They kept asking themselves, "What else can we do to keep her?" Now Blue is a wildland firefighter, doing that courageous and essential work. She's even brought her sister into an environmental career, once again demonstrating the ripple effect of this work. Blue has become an ambassador of sorts for our program, spreading the word through her talks and writings about how it can change lives.

Soon after we got into the business of putting young people on these environmental career tracks, I began to notice something: With the focus on college kids, we were leaving behind a huge number of young people whose lives were on different tracks. Just like the home economics and shop classes at my middle school were geared toward those students who were more likely headed for a career in some type of trade, there's still an enormous need to provide career opportunities for the kids who had no college plans. Luckily, there are many areas of the environmental industry where they are eager to snatch up these kids because they are so desperately in need of workers. I saw that this was a viable option for many of the young people in our Urban Youth Corps (UYC). They need to know that society hasn't given up on them; they still have hope for a stable, well-paying career. We can point these young people to environmental careers where they don't need a college diploma, in areas like wildland firefighting, wind and solar technicians, and tree-care management — doing things these young people never imagined themselves doing. For many, all they heard toward the end of high school was "What college are you going to?" — so much that it was easy for them to feel like failures if they weren't going. But when they go through our program, they see a broad expanse of opportunities. Some of them even decide to go to college after all. But whether they do or not, the environment transforms the way they see themselves. They suddenly feel like they're important because they're doing work that's important.

We didn't know much about wildland firefighting when we first stepped into this arena. With catastrophic forest fires raging without end in places like California, clearly it's a dire need we have in the nation right now. James became obsessed with the field, wondering why it wasn't something our UYC members could be doing. He began knocking on many doors. He discovered that considerable challenges were being placed in front of young people of color to prevent them from entering the field — even as it's apparent there's a critical need for more firefighters. In order to become a wildland firefighter, individuals need to obtain something known as a red card. In order to get a card, you must complete a training regimen. But it can be difficult for young people of color to get the training they need because in many places the guardians of the system are older white men who have been utilizing a good old boys network for generations to control who gets certified and therefore who can get these jobs. We've been experiencing difficulty getting access to the training for some of our young people, which makes it difficult for them to get the necessary certification. But we're not giving up. We're not going to let them cut off an entire future generation of wildland firefighters with ignorance and close-mindedness — especially when a new workforce is so needed at this time.

Sometimes being unable to secure a job has been a boon to the creative energies of our young people. When we were starting out and some of them didn't have a job waiting for them at the end of their training, we decided to include an entrepreneurial component to the training. Atiba Jones, our former Urban Youth Corps Program Manager, was so passionate about making sure these young men and women had all the tools necessary for success that he began to incorporate entrepreneurial skills in their training modules. We were thrilled when several young ladies, after being trained in historic preservation through a partnership with the National Trust for Historic Preservation, got together and started a company they called 3 Girls and a Paintbrush when they weren't successful in finding a job after working at the Martin Luther King Jr. site. They took the matter into their own hands, using the skills they had developed. Now they are businesswomen running their own enterprise (albeit on the side) … answering to no one.

James and I happened to be at a symposium where we heard representatives of the tree care industry say they were so desperate for workers that they were going to other countries and paying for people to get visas to come to the US to work for them. They moaned that they were actually losing contracts because they didn't have enough workers. We looked at each other with our eyes widened. Ding, ding, ding! We had been looking for more industries that would be open to employing many of the young people coming out of the Urban Youth Corps. It felt like a perfect fit: They have unfilled jobs; we have people that need jobs. We decided to go to the tree care companies and get them involved in the training program we were devising. We created a 10-week program during which industry experts trained them in the hard skills like tree climbing, stump grinding, grounds work, etc. Then we stepped in and trained them in soft skills like financial literacy, professional development, nutrition, conflict resolution, etiquette, cultural awareness, and attaining GEDs if they didn't have high-school diplomas. When they were ready to graduate from the program, the employers came in and conducted speed rounds of interviews. Many of our young people were hired on the spot. The last time I checked, our job rate for this field was at 97 percent for program graduates. Our next challenge overall is to make sure they stay in these jobs. This work is extremely challenging mainly because we do not have the resources to change their environment — where they live and recreate.

Recently I was driving down an Atlanta street and came upon a tree company doing work by the side of the road. It's become my habit to scan the workers as I drive by. My heart quickened when I saw dreadlocks I thought I recognized. Was that Aaron Jacobs? When I looked closer, I confirmed that it was indeed one of our guys. In fact, he was a guy I recruited myself during a Sprouts grocery shopping trip. We had an intriguing conversation while he was packing my bags.

"Oh my God, he's actually working!" I said out loud. I was so proud, like a giddy mom; it was like a visual affirmation of many months of hard work by a lot of people.

We've been getting back positive reports from the companies — Davey Tree, Bartlett Tree, Arborguard Tree Specialists, and Boutte Tree Company for the most part — but there have been hiccups for sure. These might be expected when you're sending a group of young people into an environment and culture to which they previously had no exposure. Some of the companies have actually asked us to stay involved when they've had challenges with issues like punctuality and accountability. We can understand their frustrations, but it raises a

vital question for us: How long do we stay involved? Might our continued presence be used as a crutch for some of these twenty-somethings?
If you know your mama is always going to wake you up on time in the
morning, then you never have to worry about setting the alarm clock
yourself, right? We don't think it's appropriate for us to be calling these
young men and women in the morning and asking, "Are you up now?
You've got to go to work." So, in some cases, we've decided to take a
step back and let them work out their real-world problems for themselves, in effect cutting the apron strings. But I realize that sometimes
that will lead to failure — after all, most of them are still living in the
same communities that caused them to get off-track in the first place.
Researchers and sociologists have been debating terms like "the culture
of poverty" for decades. I'm not going to pretend we have discovered
the magic bullet to answer all of those questions, but I have determined
we have to be careful of "mission creep." Is it our job to find these young
people viable careers in the environmental sphere, or to teach them
about the value of work? If we decide we're going to try to step in and
tackle the negative effects of poverty and racial oppression, where does
it end? And who's going to fund that? Some of the foundations that
provide us with generous grants, like the Kendeda Fund and Turner
Foundation, understand that we will need to invest some dollars in
training young people from challenging backgrounds, but they still
want to see results.

In acknowledgment of these vital questions, we have started something we call GYFTED — Greening Youth Foundation Trained,
Educated and Developed — where we work with young people on the
soft skills they will need in the workplace. I have been encouraged by
them and their motivation to change the trajectory of their lives. Many
have had encounters with the law, which is expected when you see statistics on the staggering percentage of black men who get arrested at
some point in their lives (as many as a third, according to some studies). But what I have found noteworthy is that they all want to turn
around the negativity and become positive, contributing members of
society. All they have to do is glance around their communities — or

in their own families — and see the sad, broken-down state that so many black men eventually wind up in. They don't want to be derelicts or menaces or whatever other labels society is quick to slap on them. Our job at GYF becomes figuring out the formula to help them avoid that fate, to assist them in stepping out of the vicious cycle that entraps so many of their peers.

We have a different set of challenges with many of our young ladies, often connected to the babies that so many of them have at home. We were stunned when we saw how many of them would fail to show up for work because they didn't have childcare.

"Oh, don't have a babysitter," they would say when we inquired about their absence.

"So you just didn't come? Didn't you know yesterday that you didn't have a babysitter?"

At one point, we seriously considered opening up a daycare center at our training site. But we stepped back from that idea; it was too close to mission creep. What we have done is start to partner with nonprofits that provide childcare. But you really have to learn when to stay in your lane because these issues can begin to mushroom and take over your entire program.

In addition to all our work to prepare the young people, it's also necessary for the sites to take their own steps to reach out to them. I will talk about this in greater detail in the chapter about changing the culture, but if this whole endeavor is going to be successful, it is absolutely essential for efforts to be made on the other side. I was tickled by one ranger in particular who demonstrated how he was able to connect to the young people in a most unusual way. It occurred in the mountains of California, where this ranger was having difficulty connecting with the group of mostly African Americans he was charged with managing. One day he came upon the young men in a room, listening to music and doing dances that were popular at the time. The ranger saw this and said, "Oh, I can do that."

"Yeah, *sure* you can!" they responded, laughing at this burly bearded white park ranger.

What they didn't know was that he was actually on a break dancing team in high school and he could really dance, despite his looks. When he bust a move, the guys went crazy, falling onto the floor and screaming at the top of their lungs. They couldn't believe it. The video they took of his moves quickly gathered a large enthusiastic following on social media. After that moment, the ranger had no difficulty connecting with these young men. He now uses the incident in talks he gives about the importance of cultural sensitivity. This middle-aged white man found a way to connect to these young black men through music and dance; it immediately led to many other connections between them and a much smoother working relationship. He took a chance and was intentional about reaching out to them, even if there were some risks that he might be perceived as going too far. I'm not advising that white people should go out and learn how to break-dance to connect to black youth, but it is incumbent upon white managers to try to find some avenue of connection if the organization is going to bring those young people into that arena. Do some investigation. Find commonalities. This is a message that I think should be spread all across corporate America, the private sector, the public sector — anywhere that people of color are stepping into areas where previously they might not have been welcomed. It may not be easy or comfortable, but it must be done. In the environmental field, where we are about to face enormous shortages of workers, we have no choice. Eventually, if we have our way at GYF, in the near future we will have more people of color as managers.

I must pause here to share the story of April Baldwin, a history major from Tuskegee University when she first started with us in February 2015. She is currently at Alabama State University working on her MA in history. In 2015, April was a Museum Collections Management Intern working at Tuskegee Institute and Airmen National Historic Site. She was a strong intern, always asking lots of questions and challenging herself to give her absolute best to the job at hand. As such, it was no surprise when we learned that in January 2016 April transitioned into a permanent position with the National Park Service as a Park Guide. I realized that GYF was providing a much-needed resource to the park system when we placed interns at the Selma to Montgomery National Historic Trail and learned that April Baldwin was their supervisor. Our work had gone full circle.

"During my time with Greening Youth, I was exposed to all aspects of the NPS," Baldwin said. "I got a chance to work in cultural resources and be out with the public doing interpretation on the weekends. The PLC hiring authority was the best edge on the application for my current job, and now, two years later, I couldn't be happier! Through this position, I've gotten to travel to the Grand Canyon and Biscayne National Park in Miami, and I even got to present at the National Postal Museum in Washington, DC. Greening Youth broadened my career options in the field of history. If it wasn't for another GYF intern randomly DM-ing me on Instagram telling me to apply for that internship, I wouldn't have the career I have today!"

CHAPTER 6

Going International

A T THE RISK OF VEERING OFF into the realm of romantic comedy, I'd like to tell you how I first connected with my business partner and the love of my life, James Ezeilo. Beyond being quite a meet-cute tale, this story is important because I'm sure that GYF would not have become what it is without his brilliant legal and business mind. So, the meeting that fateful evening in Gainesville at the University of Florida College of Law truly had global implications. (Okay, maybe I'm getting a little carried away.)

It was at the start of the second semester, January 1993, and the law school's Black Law Students Association was holding a kickoff event for the semester, giving the new black students an opportunity to meet with us veterans before the semester officially began. I was excited because I was no longer a newbie; I was one semester in! It was a month after my 23rd birthday, having graduated from Spelman College seven months earlier. My first semester of law school had been a bit overwhelming, exciting, and a little scary all at the same time. Thanks to programs like Virgil D. Hawkins for minority students, I — along with a handful of other minority students — was able to go to law school a couple of months prior to my fellow incoming first-year students to get a bit of a head start. The program was deemed necessary because research has proven that because students of color do not have as much exposure to the legal profession as their white counterparts, they have a more difficult time adapting to the demands of law school. Many white students have grown up around lawyers and judges, so hearing about a brief or even going into a courtroom is not a totally new experience for them. The program's intent was to make the already challenging experience a little more doable — removing a lot of anxiety. Virgil D. Hawkins was an inspiration to us, for his efforts in 1949 to integrate the University of Florida Law School. Mr. Hawkins was a 43-year-old man who received a letter from UF Law rejecting his application because he was African American. Mr. Hawkins would not accept the prejudiced decision and decided to file suit. His legal battle went on for nine years, laying the foundation for the integration of Florida's graduate and professional schools. While I sat in those classrooms and labored to master the grueling work, no matter how challenging it was I knew I could never give up because I was standing on the shoulders of giants who had fought battles much harder than the one facing me.

Black students at UF law school in the early 1990s knew we needed to have each other's backs if we were going to make it through the gauntlet of racial microaggressions, slights, and outright frontal attacks in one healthy piece. It would particularly cause my skin to crawl when my study group (almost always all black) would be preparing for a test and discover that somehow the white students had in their possession a class outline from the previous semester with highlighted areas for what would be on the test. Needless to say, I started being more strategic about the makeup of my study groups. At the kickoff event, students who had been at the law school for a while would get up and welcome the new students, trying to get them in the right mental space for what was to come. It was an important gathering for all of us.

I saw an empty seat near my friends and settled in to hear the speeches. There was a party scheduled for immediately after the meeting, so I was thinking about what the rest of my evening looked like, whether I had time to stop in at the party for a minute. I was living with one of my father's younger sisters, my Aunt Betty, and her husband, my Uncle Dave, who had graciously offered to let me crash with them the first year. I was wondering if I would disturb them if I came in too late. Also, did I even want to go to the after-party? I had work to do; I wanted to get a jump-start on my torts class reading. Then there was my contracts class that always required me to read over the cases a little closer because my contracts professor was a big fan of the Socratic method and I was *not* going to be embarrassed. I was in deep thought when I sensed that someone was standing next to me. I looked up and saw James Ezeilo. Admittedly I had already spotted him earlier in the event. In fact, I asked my Morehouse brother, Kendall Moore, to tell me a little about the newbie in the oxford shirt. Kendall told me that the new guy was a Florida A&M graduate and was from Florida. I responded by telling him, "I think he is the one!" Yes, I actually said that out loud. He was very attractive and captured me with his green eyes and strong stature; clearly, he was a real man. As with most of these first meeting stories, part of the narrative changes depending on which one of us is recounting it. James says that I intentionally stole his seat. I'll admit that I was trying to play coy. I could tell James was accustomed to women cooing over him.

"Excuse me," he said. "Um, I was sitting there." He pointed to a backpack that was sitting next to the chair, which I hadn't noticed until that moment.

"Were you really?" I said. "I don't see your name on it."

I called myself being flirtatious. But much later, when we went back through the story, James said he thought I was actually being mean. Guys never get it, do they? I mean, didn't he ever get hit by a girl when he was little? Not always knowing the best way to express our emotions when we are little — especially when we like a boy — we resort to being rough. Of course, this doesn't explain why I still used these tactics as a grown-ass woman. In fact, I still find that I (gently) hit, pinch, and bite those that I love. Is that weird? I may need some therapy over this, now that I think about it.

I have to admit, I was more than intrigued by this handsome stranger. I made up my mind that I was definitely hitting up the after-party. As we were leaving the gathering and heading to the party, I leaned into a friend of mine and gestured toward James.

"I like that one!" I said to her in a stage whisper. We both giggled as we walked out of the room together.

James and I sent furtive glances in each other's direction at the party. And then Kendall brought James over to me.

"I wanted to introduce you two," he said.

We told him we had already met. Kinda. At this point James began to see that I was not as snippy as he first thought. He asked me to dance, so we moved it to the section of the room that had been cleared as a dance floor. The room was kinda dark. I think we were in the guest house of one of the third-year (3L) students. I remember there being a strobe light. So, the mood was very contrived. All of the 1Ls were lined up against the wall trying to make small talk with one another while the upper classmen were having a good time — at our expense, I'm sure. As we worked it out on the dance floor to some of those golden jams from the early 1990s, I was trying not to stare at James or any of the other dudes in the room.

"Are you a model?" he asked, with a kindly smile. I saw the twinkle in his green eyes. I wanted to laugh at the line, but when I looked in his face, I saw that he was serious. He was proud of his smoothness. So I took it easy on him and played along.

"Well, thank you, but no — I'm a law student. Thank you for the compliment, though."

When I tease James about that line, his handy rejoinder is always, "But it worked, didn't it?" I guess he's right about that. But not before he almost screwed the whole thing up.

I gave him my phone number that night, thinking that perhaps this might be the start of something interesting. However, James never called me. For about two months. So, he slipped from my mind. *His loss!* I thought to myself, with more than a little attitude.

One day I was walking out of the Lawton Chiles Library, rushing as usual to get to class. I looked up and saw James heading toward me. He smiled at me, but I could tell he was a bit embarrassed.

"You never called me," I said, getting right to the point.

James apologized. He told me he was still trying to figure out the law school terrain, and he meant no slight whatsoever. He was so cute that I forgave him on the spot. We decided that we didn't want to get into a serious relationship, but we both could use a study partner. So that's what we did; we began to study together. Everything was totally platonic. At first. We were just two black law students helping each other deal with the bullshit. But I'm sure you won't be surprised to hear that we began to realize there was a strong attraction between us. Studying together was not going to suffice.

When I look back on my childhood, it's easy to see why I was intrigued by James. Both of my parents were products of the South — Mom in Georgia and Dad in Virginia — who had moved up North and in the 1960s became entranced by the emerging Black Power movement. They quickly embraced the movement's emphasis on black self-love and teaching black people in America about the brilliance and power of their ancestors, who had developed sophisticated medicines, architecture, and mathematics long before other civilizations in the world. By the time I came along in 1970, their record shop and bookstore in Jersey City, called The Magic Id — named after Freud's part of the psyche that controls pleasure — was a local hangout and hotspot for everybody from prominent musicians to Black Panthers. From day one, I was absorbing their teachings about the glory of Africa. At one point my father even owned a small fuel company that imported fuel from Nigeria and sold it to black families in surrounding neighborhoods to heat their homes. I guess I was being preprogrammed for an attraction to someone like James. He was like a perfect melding of two worlds: He had come to the United States from Nigeria when he was only three; although he had a strong identification with his native land and has an influential family back home, he had spent nearly his entire life in the US. Culturally he was just as much African American as he was African. He was able to provide me a peek into a culture about which I had a deep curiosity, but he also understood the culture in which I had been immersed my whole life.

James and I got married in May 1995. In a flash of inspiration, we decided to get married the same week we graduated from law school, since all of our family members would be gathered already. Now that

I'm looking back 24 years later, I can't imagine what madness had descended over us. With our plan, our families had to race from the Gainesville, Florida, graduation over the course of 36 hours back to Atlanta for a rather large wedding celebration. Insanity. I break out in hives even thinking about that weekend. But somehow it all worked out, quite beautifully.

James and I in those early years embarked on several business ventures together. We built an entire village of vendors to sell wares at the 1996 Olympics in Atlanta. We started a business offering low-cost legal services for things like divorce and bankruptcy — services that typically were beyond the reach of poor folks. Our ventures always had a common basis: their primary intent, much more than making money, was to serve our people.

One day over a decade ago, on a neighborhood walk with Ruth Kitchen, a lovely white woman who lived across the street, we began talking about how schoolchildren are taught little about the environment. Ruth was a former teacher, while I had been working in the environmental world for years, so we were approaching the issue from two different directions. But we came to the same conclusion: we needed to do something about this. I shared with her the reaction I had from teaching an Earth Day lesson to my youngest son's kindergarten class, making it fun and interactive. So the idea blossomed with Ruth to start some type of business going into schools to teach students about the environment and their responsibility to protect it. But where to start? At the time, James was running his own law firm, racing back and forth every week between our new home in Georgia and Newark, where he had a full complement of associates, paralegals, and secretaries. He would know what we needed to do.

We found James out back, cleaning the pool.

"James, what legal structure should we make this whole thing that we're going to call Greening Youth Foundation?" I asked him.

With that simple question, an incredible decade-plus odyssey was begun. It has been a thrilling endeavor — exciting and fulfilling. Early on, James stepped in to help me forge a solid business model. "This is great," he said at the time, "but how do we also make it sustainable? How do we make sure it makes money so we can continue doing this in the future?"

It was a crucial question for us to confront early on because I think that's the point where too many nonprofits falter. They begin with great worthwhile missions, but they don't have the vision to keep it financially sustainable. They're usually started by a person with a passion, but not a business background. With me and James, we were able to marry the two — literally — a combination that has helped us flourish into a multimillion-dollar organization.

In 2012 we began to think about taking our work to Africa. We connected with Christa Sanders, my dear Spelman classmate who was the Global Director for New York University (NYU), based in Ghana. Christa needed an environmental program that the NYU students traveling abroad could participate in. The mission in Ghana was similar to the US: engage underrepresented young people and transform them into environmental stewards while also introducing them to a wide range of environmental careers. The mission was even more intense in Africa not only because of the incredible vibrancy and importance of the environment there but also the extreme peril it is facing. We were aware of the long and troubling history of nations outside of this continent swooping down and pilfering an abundance of its natural resources — with little benefit to the locals. When James's dad became ill and we traveled to Nigeria, we had many revelations. As we began to learn more about what was happening on the ground in Africa, we realized that we could have a bigger impact there than we ever thought.

James Ezeilo, CEO, GYF West Africa

Once I got immersed in the environmental world in the US, I looked at what was going on in Nigeria with a strategic eye. When Angelou and I traveled to states within Nigeria outside of the economic centers like Lagos, I began to realize that this was the land that the environmental movement forgot. We spend so much time in the US concerning ourselves with small-scale questions, like whether we can remember to bring the recyclable bags with us on our next trip to the grocery store, but in Africa it sometimes feels like the environmental movement has made a conscious decision to leapfrog over the continent and pretend it's not even there.

This feels directly connected to the Western world's traditional relationship with Africa — extract as many natural resources as possible, on unbelievably epic scales, then walk away from the continent and say, "Um, you can take it from here." We saw vast swaths of land that had been clear-cut, then planted with species that shouldn't even be growing in Africa — introducing all manner of invasive varieties that were doing their own job of steadily wiping out more forests. Entities primarily from Asia and Europe had taken what they wanted and left the residents on their own trying to figure out how to repair

James's 50ᵗʰ birthday celebration
on Lagos Beach in Nigeria.
Credit: Jameelah Wilhoite

the damage. But most of these regions don't have the scientists and environmental engineers with the necessary skill sets to accomplish this. The problems are so enormous that you must make a scary existential decision: Do you find a way to go back to square one, teaching residents and young people all about recycling and water conservation and reducing their footprint — issues that GYF has been engaging young people with in the US over the past decade — or do you create a new model that can fix as much of the damage as physically possible?

When we began to think about working in Africa, we initially decided to try the first approach. We talked to local leaders and non-governmental organizations (NGOs), attempting to assess where their thinking was on the environmental problems the continent needed to overcome. We were quite disturbed by their responses. Essentially, most of these entities had no appetite to even have the discussion because the problems were just too enormous to tackle. We had become accustomed to a model where we identified a problem, came up with the behavioral changes that would help eliminate or alleviate the problem, then figured out how to convince the public to change its behavior. We saw that, with the right approach, we might be able to convince a large section of the public to become better environmental stewards — and if we started early enough, we could help young people forge lifetime behaviors that would ultimately benefit everyone.

But when you come across a river in Africa that is so overwhelmed with garbage and plastic that you almost can't believe your eyes, what can you do? You ask yourself, "How in the world will that ever get cleaned up?" It's mind-boggling. Right away, you know we're far past the point of saying, "Let's come out on Saturdays and pick up trash, and let's use fewer plastic bottles." The problem is so enormous, so overpowering, that you become paralyzed; you don't even know where to start. And that's precisely how most of the African residents feel. In recent years, as the economy has thrived and the population has continued to grow, most individuals conclude that the problem is too large for their personal behavior to have any effect — so they just go ahead and throw that plastic bottle into the river.

We had to figure out the best way that we could have an effect. Early on, we saw that if we were going to make any inroads, our message needed to have a jobs component. The unemployment rate in Nigeria at the end of 2018 was 23.10 percent, according to data compiled by the World Bank. Clearly, there is a significant need in the country for jobs, jobs, jobs. If you're not talking to them about projects that will include jobs, they're not going to be listening. Their thinking is going to sound something like — If I can't feed my kids and get enough for their school fees, then this whole alternative cook stove that you're talking about that's better for the environment — so what?

We got an important taste of what we were up against when we thought we could try to do something about the water sachet bags that are used in most countries in West Africa for drinking water. From a Western perspective, basically they're the West African version of the water bottles that have become ubiquitous in the US, both stemming from similar concerns about the cleanliness of the local drinking water. The sachets are little plastic bags, roughly the size of a Ziploc sandwich bag, that get filled with water at local purification stations. They are sold for pennies, making them accessible to most of the population, much cheaper than the water bottles that might cost up to 50 times more. Laborers, construction workers, anybody who might need some water during the course of the day will bite off a little piece of the bag, drink the water, and toss it wherever they happen to be standing, littering the streets, the waterways, everything in sight. What I find ironic is that some of the sachets are actually produced by large European and US multinationals companies, but they hide their involvement by using secondary or tertiary subsidiaries so you won't know it's them unless you do some corporate excavation. They realize how much of an environmental challenge is caused by their bags; it's bad enough that you see discarded Coke bottles scattered everywhere you turn.

I should add that the Nigerian government makes a concerted effort to clean up most areas of the major cities like Lagos, where American, European, and Asian business people will spend most of their time. The same is true in Ghana. In Ikoyi or Victoria Island in Lagos, we've seen this workforce of thousands of women picking up these sachet bags and other garbage, a 4 AM swarm removing litter on sidewalks and highways before dawn breaks. The government has turned cleaning up these high-traffic tourist areas into a huge job vehicle — something GYF discovered when we launched an initiative to encourage people to recycle the sachets. We tried to tailor our message to the young people, encouraging their indignation over the perils the sachets were presenting to the local environment. But we got hard pushback from their moms and dads. The kids would go home and say, "Mom, Dad, don't buy those bags. They're bad." But they would get dismissive responses from the parents, for whom the bags made much more economic sense than the alternatives, such as the American-made bottled water from Nestlé or Coke. In addition, the bags were another job source, providing income to huge numbers of vendors that sold them to make a living. In effect, by trying to stop the use of the bags, we were imperiling the future of an entire industry. We had to figure out how to talk about environmental challenges in a way that wouldn't impact the region's economy and people's ability to eat. When you can't eat, somehow the fact that the rivers are being clogged by plastic drops way down on your list of pressing priorities.

We took several steps back and started to think on a much larger scale. First of all, Africa is incredibly important to the global environment. As Nobel laureate Dr. Wangari Maathai of Kenya demonstrated to the world, African trees play a huge role in combating the effects of excessive carbon emissions around the planet — emissions we already know are much greater in the developed nations than they are in Africa itself. Africa essentially is the world's lungs. But that realization has not been embraced by the environmental community in a meaningful way. So, when we look at gatherings like the Paris Accord and the Kyoto Protocol, when all the big boys come together to discuss the future of climate change and how we can slow it down — nobody even talks about reducing it anymore; we're way past that — interestingly, developing nations are not really part of the discussions, but are asked to sign on to the resulting agreements. This is despite the scientifically acknowledged fact that African trees can help the world keep breathing. I often asked myself why they're over here doubling down on emissions in Denmark, one of the greenest places on the planet, or starting yet another project in Paris, which is so advanced, while ignoring African trees? But as I got deeper into the weeds, I started to understand why — because in Europe they are preaching to the choir without having to make any adjustments to the sermon. You get a lot of enthusiastic nods around the table to your every word. You are operating in an echo chamber. But when you step onto the African continent, you have to come with some game. The issues are so distinct, the audience so different, you need to conceive a new strategy — a strong, long-term one — that must bring about immediate returns and yet be a sustainable platform for the next 5, 10, or even 50 years. If you come to the African people with a strategy that does not include jobs and growth and helping countries become self-sustaining, you will be voted out of office with the next election cycle.

The NGOs working in Africa seem to be following a different playbook than they use in the US, where they are held to high standards. There they have parameters they must respect — if they step too far away from them, they'll wind up on the front page of the *New York Times* or the *Wall Street Journal*. There are significant checks and balances that don't exist in Africa. They'll get funding from USAID, they'll get funding from the World Bank, they'll go into a country on the continent and implement something, then they'll disappear. They don't seem to have to meet the same ethical standards or answer the same questions from the funding entities that they must answer in the US. There's little accountability or requirement to show return on investment. *How did you help the people on the ground?* The question is never asked. There's nobody stepping to them and saying, "You did these five things that you said you were going to do. Now show me the results."

In the absence of oversight, too many of these entities revert to human nature: greed. I was startled and more than a little disappointed when I began asking a lot of questions of NGOs in Africa and getting troubling answers. But then again, I shouldn't have been surprised. After all, it's the same relationship that the Western world has had with the continent for centuries — extract resources and then disappear. What I discovered was that, in the developing world, they had created a way to turn conservation, the world's desperate desire to preserve our planet, into a revenue stream.

GYF first asked of ourselves a basic question: Where can we add value? What can we do in a space that we're comfortable in and that's going to have an impact long-term on the continent? We figured that we could either do something that'll make a small splash or we could just go for it and go big. We chose the second option.

We stepped into an area that's known as carbon trading. We began by examining existing projects on the continent and seeing how we might improve the models previously used, perhaps by partnering with other NGOs that were successfully implementing projects. However, what we kept seeing was that all these ventures would start, get to a certain point, and fizzle out. In trying to figure out which ones were successful, we compiled lists of these projects that just didn't do much. It was quite odd; I couldn't figure out what was going on.

We settled on a simple yet powerful idea: Let's plant trees. Not a big deal, right? Trees are great; they help combat carbon emissions and make the world's lungs even more powerful. We approached Edo State in Nigeria, and its governor loved the idea. The concept was to plant 100,000 trees in Edo State, which used to be a large timber region. While trees sound like a simple answer to carbon emissions, they're not exactly coveted by developers. In a battle for which entity will have domain over the land, the trees or the developers, the developers almost always win. But after finding an area of forest reserves that could work, we mapped out a plan to plant 100,000 trees. My first step was to find funding, so I began knocking on the doors of likely foundations. A Paris-based one with a history of planting trees in Africa was enthusiastic about our plan — with one caveat: Our 100,000 target wasn't large enough.

"If you can do 200,000, that'd be even better," they told us.

That was not a response I was expecting. "If you give us the money, we'll plant 200,000 trees," I said.

For some reason, I started to get curious at that point. Actually, suspicious might be a more accurate word. Why were they so motivated to give us all this money, just for trees? What were they getting out of it? I've never been the shy sort, so I asked.

"Why? Why are you giving money to these places for trees? What's in it for you?"

Traditionally that's not the kind of question you ask a funder when they are handing you a wad of cash. Their answer was entirely unsatisfying to me. It sounded coy, vague, like they didn't want to give me a real answer. Prompted by their coyness, I dug further into this foundation's model and background. *What exactly were they up to here?*

I was even more adamant when told they would give me the money to plant the trees but I'd have to be responsible for monitoring them for at least a decade. That meant I would need another pot of money. I asked the foundation, "How do I deal with that second part? Can you point me in the right direction?"

"Well, you'd have to work with the government to get assurances," they said. "Why don't we talk later when you get a few more pieces in place?"

It was an odd model to me, that they were so interested in the planting but not the maintenance. What I discovered was that, in the carbon trading system, companies take advantage of a verification platform that attaches a carbon credit price tag to the planting of trees. Depending on how many acres you were planting and how long you were going to allow those trees to exist, a third-party verifier could say, "That's worth X amount of tons of carbon emissions that are going to be removed from the atmosphere. So this project is worth X millions of dollars." The companies were then taking those millions of dollars in carbon credits and using them to offset the tax liability they were being hit with in Europe — a continent that is heavily committed to cap and trade.

The more I dug, the more stunned I was by these arrangements. What was even more stunning was that nobody was tracking the number of carbon trading projects that were being created. Africa was a prime location for these because of its vast amounts of available land and the fragmented, disjointed nature of its infrastructure. These are countries that are not talking to each other, so you can do projects in Liberia, in South Africa, in the Congo, and none of them will know the other projects exist. The countries got the trees out of the deal, but when they received the funding to plant the trees, they were signing over their rights to any future carbon credits for the project. But they got the trees, so they weren't even investigating any further. They didn't get money to maintain the trees, but they also knew that in five or ten years, whatever the amount of time they agreed upon, they could cut them down and make money from the harvest. They were excited by the deal because they were getting a future crop. But what they weren't realizing was that they had just signed away what could be many millions of dollars in carbon credits.

We decided we wanted to insert ourselves into this equation. If the European corporations could profit from the carbon trading, we thought it was only fair for them to share some of that profit with the African nations that were making these millions possible. Our plan was to go to countries like Liberia, Congo, and Nigeria and tell them we would find the funding to plant and maintain the trees, but we would take the additional step of going to the same third-party verifiers the Europeans were using and hiring them to put a price tag on the amount of carbon credits for each of our projects. Then GYF would take a small percentage as a consulting fee — allowing us to get back all our money that we put up front for planting and maintaining the trees — and the millions remaining would go straight to the African nation. They would get enough money to build an internal workforce that could develop the skill sets to step into a wide range of environmental careers like forest rangers. We could bring in the best trainers in the US industry and transfer all that knowledge to the continent.

We took the additional step of creating a database of every carbon trading project on the continent, almost like the equivalent of a stock exchange that can track the money and the equity flowing back and forth. After we partnered with Brigham Young University — Angelou met the director of a Brigham Young University research center at an Ashoka Conference — to help us create the database, by the second or third meeting, these young people were shocked by what they found. These smart kids at this somewhat right-leaning institution were telling us, "Oh my God, we didn't know this was going on!" It's been an incredible education for them. We checked in with the World Bank, which is supposed to be controlling all of the carbon credits in the world right now, and we found only two projects supposedly in existence in Africa — a tiny one in Cote d'Ivoire and possibly one being created in South Africa. That was it. But we'd already identified more than 130 projects, which we're putting on a website for the world to be able to access. I'm not going to speculate why the World Bank is only informing the public of two projects, but clearly there's a whole lot more happening behind the scenes — hundreds of millions of dollars of value being created with African soil.

Such a database we hope will be a game-changer for African nations, who will come to the table with far more information than they had in the past — and the ability to share in the value being created with their land. We envision the creation of a whole new green market, one in which many more parties will see financial benefit besides a handful of European multinationals. In the process, the entire planet profits because many millions more trees will be planted in Africa, thus strengthening the world's lungs. After the rest of the world has used Africa as a free and easy pot of money and natural resources for generations, raping the land and taking what they wished, I think it's about time that the continent turned the tables a bit.

GYF is discovering different avenues for communities of color to play a part in this emerging green economy in the US and abroad, West Africa in particular. Whether we are educating youth about the importance of being environmental stewards, training urban youth to obtain certifications in natural resource fields that have been historically white, teaching entrepreneurial skills to young adults, or exposing college students to careers in the environmental sector, the end result is bringing a new voice to an industry that is in desperate need of innovation.

CHAPTER 7

Changing the Culture

IT HAS BEEN FASCINATING for me to see how quickly the landscape has shifted in the spaces where GYF does most of our work in the US. When first starting out, we actually approached organizations that did internships with the federal parks and lands, seeing if they wanted to hire us to help them diversify their pool of interns because it typically was exclusively white. We got a lot of polite "No thank you" responses. In retrospect, those responses proved to be the impetus we needed to create our own thriving workforce of youth of color.

Now that we've become a strong force in the internship space ourselves, sending hundreds of black, Latinx, and Native American young people into parks across the country, we've had some of those same organizations approaching us proffering the same arrangement we were offering them in the beginning, namely, that they outsource their recruitment of diverse youth to GYF. "We'll put a line item in our budget and work with GYF to do diversity recruiting," they'll say to us.

Our response? "No thank you."

We're often competing with these organizations to win *entire* projects — and often winning the contracts. So why would we now be content to be a line item in their budgets? But I think they're trying to get a little taste of the GYF secret sauce — and perhaps take us out of the competition at the same time. We made a pivotal decision early on that has turned out to be incredibly fortuitous. When we turned down the offer to be a diversity subcontractor for these white organizations, they were putting big sums of money on the table, money that was looking quite enticing for our new foundation that was still worried about bringing in enough cash to keep going. We knew if we decided to do it for one, we would have a hard time justifying not doing it for other organizations that approached us. But we'd be putting ourselves in a box. The choice was quite stark: Become an outsource for the big companies or aspire to be a big company that has the one thing that the rest of them don't have — a diverse workforce. In other words, take the quick money and in the process play ourselves small, or hold out and say no to the money. We chose the second route, but we didn't stop there. We looked at what these bigger organizations were doing and incorporated that into our model so that we could then compete for the big contracts.

Once we turned down the subcontracting route, we had another crucial decision to make: Do we try to become a big foundation that brings in all kids, or do we retain our focus on underrepresented youth? We had some intense internal debates over this with our leadership team and our board. But James in particular was adamant: "Let's say we work with diverse youth. That's what we do. And then we drop the mic."

We knew we would get some pushback for being so explicit about it. Although it wasn't that long ago, most foundations back then were not comfortable defining themselves by race. First of all, is it even legal — can we come right out and say that? Since James and I both came from the legal world, we dissected that approach and saw no reason why we couldn't. It was our mission, our reason for being.

In 2008, a dramatic historical event shocked the world and dramatically changed our fortunes — the election of Barack Obama. His administration ushered in a major initiative, America's Great Outdoors, to diversify all of the federal agencies. Obama directed his secretaries to focus on diversity in a way that the federal government had never done before. Not only did he mandate that his agencies focus more on connecting young people to the outdoors and reaching out to more diverse groups, he also issued annual reports on their progress.

Nothing moves a public agency more than knowing they will be publicly assessed and graded every year. Right away, we saw a whole lot of scrambling going on inside these federal agencies, as they realized they hadn't built an infrastructure that would enable them to recruit more youth of color. Where could they find black and Latinx kids who were interested in the outdoors, who would want to spend the entire summer working in a national park? They had no idea. All at once, GYF popped up on all their radar screens. Suddenly, we were holding the Willy Wonka golden ticket.

The federal agencies needed to make serious progress in this area, and quickly, so their needs aligned perfectly with GYF's mission. That decision we had just made to define ourselves by saying we worked with diverse youth proved to be incredibly prescient. When these agencies wanted to know how to diversify their pool of young people, they called us, asking: "How do we talk to them? How do we engage them? Can you pull together a group of diverse young people to work on this project?"

We noticed that the big foundations that had been doing this work for decades with white kids started creating diversity departments. And they started asking for our help. But it was too late for that. We didn't need them anymore. The buzz around the country was to have these diverse youth engaged in projects, and we just happened to have thousands of them at our disposal. James and I jokingly recalled that scene in Spike Lee's *Malcolm X* movie, when Malcolm is confronted by the police in front of the hospital and with a point of his finger directs dozens of the Fruit of Islam to march away, all in perfect lockstep. We felt like we had that level of trust and loyalty from these young people, who knew that we love them and would do anything to protect them. When I read the testimonials from the young people who have gone on to gratifying careers in this sector, such as park rangers for the National Park Service, they often talk about how unaware they were that such careers even existed, but they placed their trust in GYF and their lives were transformed. A few years ago, I did a lecture series, called "The New Face of Conservation," at Spelman

College in Atlanta, my alma mater, and I implored the young ladies from Spelman and their counterparts from Morehouse to investigate environmental career possibilities to get ahead of the coming wave. I don't want us to repeat the mistakes we made with the dot-com boom, where we undoubtedly arrived late to the game, after the teams had been divvied up and all the players chosen. We were like the awkward unathletic kid watching from the sidelines, begging somebody to let us play for a couple of minutes. Quite a few of the ladies from Spelman actually came over and worked with us, so I guess my words resonated with them.

I do a lot of speaking on college campuses, and I've been struck by how quickly things are changing in the world of young people. At many colleges, they can even major in something called environmental studies now, where they delve into many of the questions I spend much of my days pondering. The opportunities in the field are abounding, everywhere I turn. And as with most major change, young people are going to be on the leading edge. Hopefully my generation won't have done so much damage by the time they're in charge that they can't save this beautiful planet of ours.

As we moved beyond the federal government and started working with the private sector, we learned we had to move differently in that space. At first we thought the drill would be the same: they let us know what they're looking for, we provide them with a pool of applicants, they select, we manage. We have it so well-honed that it's as sharp as the tip of a knife. But we started getting questions we had never heard before. We realized we had been naïve in thinking we could work from the same playbook. (My sons will be proud of me for my command of the sports metaphors.) Normally when we provide a pool of applicants, the federal agencies would take our word for it that they all were qualified and appropriate for the job. We'd give them five and they'd pick two or three. But that didn't work with the private sector. They wanted so much more: How many times had we reached out to the different applicants? What was the conversation like with each one? What are their personal interests? What are their hobbies? We were stunned, trying to figure out what these companies were looking for — and why they didn't just take our word for it that these applicants would be fine. Why did they care about all these intangibles?

What we eventually realized is that they were thinking about their corporate culture. They knew it might be a shock to the system of many of these kids; they wanted to know who might be most likely to fit in. They kept asking us to come visit their corporate headquarters: Come out to Oregon. Come out to Denver. Spend time with us. Come out to our campus in California and see what our culture is like.

And usually there was a tinge of worry underlying their requests. They knew they were bringing in a different entity than they were used to, somebody who came from different places than where they usually recruited, with different backgrounds and interests. This was conspicuously different than their usual hiring process: they'd reach out to a colleague, a sister, a friend, and just perpetuate this cycle of everyone looking the same, thinking the same, enjoying the same holidays. So here we were, trying to bring in this unicorn, and they're like, "Whoa, first you have to come and look around because you're a unicorn, too." Finally, James took them up on the invitation, and he visited one of their corporate headquarters. There's no need for me to identify the particular company; it could be any one of a dozen. They sat him down for hours and threw a barrage of questions at him. At some point, it dawned on James what was going on: they were trying to find a comfort level. They still weren't comfortable with us. They needed to spend unstructured time with us, just to see what it felt like. When we finally did send them an intern, their enthusiasm was so over the top, even that was troubling to me. It sounded like a script we had heard before with our interns and had a theme can be summed up in one word: surprise. They just couldn't believe how personable and well-spoken the intern was. It's a response I've been getting for decades. After attending an all-white boarding school and a predominantly white law school, I know how to code switch with the best of them. Still, I will get the surprised responses, white people coming up to me after a speech and crowing that I "speak so well."

These companies wanted to get the same intern for their next internship, and the one after that; they were afraid to risk somebody else, even though we kept reassuring them that we had plenty more. That's when I realized we had to back up and look at this from a different angle. On both sides, we needed to study each other, figure out each other, see how each other walked and breathed and moved. In many ways, that process is a microcosm for the entire movement: the need for the white environmental world to become comfortable including communities of color in each step of the movement and the necessity for communities of color to understand that there will be some initial awkward moments as we learn to see and trust each other. I can get as frustrated or impatient as I want, but that's not going to help the process or accelerate the learning and understanding that needs to happen.

One of the companies took it a step further: They asked if they could actually accompany us on a college tour, to see how we "engaged" with the young people that we recruited to be interns. They wanted to see us in action. After a bit of hesitation, we agreed. I wasn't going on the tour, but we let them accompany our project managers as they toured several HBCUs. I saw the posts that our people were putting up on social media during the tour, so from the outside, I got the impression that things were going well. They were driving from one campus to the next. We had a bit of a disagreement in the beginning because the company wanted the GYF folks to wear their gear; that didn't work for us. We said it was a GYF college tour that we had invited them to participate in; further we had the relationship with the HBCUs. They wound up going to about 10 different colleges. After I saw social media posts at the first few, I began to notice there were no white people in the pictures. Where were the outdoor retailer reps?

When it was over, the company came back to us and announced, "That didn't really work for us." They actually bowed out of the project altogether. After all of that planning, they decided it was a no-go for them. It was somewhat head-spinning for me. I asked myself, "What just happened?"

When our project managers returned after the tour, they said they were trying really hard to engage the company reps, with no success. When they waded into the college lunchroom where all the students were eating and they made their pitch about GYF internships, they would try to include the company reps in the discussion, but the reps wouldn't really participate. "Hey, we have all these internships available," the project manager would say. "Why don't you come shout at me? We're going to be in the hallway doing impromptu interviews." Then he'd look up and see the retailer rep standing sheepishly in the corner. The project managers would work to set up platforms for the retailer reps to interact, but they did not really participate. They just weren't comfortable.

I never really got feedback from the company about what caused them to step back. But in the end, it was clear to me that there's a lot more work to be done. I naively thought it'd be easy — after all, these retailers are in the business of selling things, and they're currently missing out on selling to a huge swath of our population. So, I thought they'd be eager to dive in and engage with our population, facilitated by GYF. But that's not what happened. I realized that it's going to take a lot longer than I thought to change their cultures enough that they're comfortable with us. Our team has gone back to the drawing board to give it more thought. Perhaps we don't start with interns; maybe there's another way to start the engagement process with these companies. Maybe we offer a tiered approach starting with sourcing résumés.

I have colleagues who run environmental groups focusing on people of color, and they tell me that these companies are all too eager to partner with them. But those partnerships typically involve the companies giving them products. They donate jackets and water bottles and all this stuff, and that's where the engagement will end. But I think the reason why GYF is different, why things get a lot more complicated with us and we have difficulty creating the same smooth relationship, is because we're actually saying we want to effectuate change. We want to transform your workforce. That's too close. That's a lot different than "Here's 10 jackets. Enjoy!" Instead, we're asking them to welcome somebody into their workforce who is different than all the other workers they have hired. We're telling them, "Hey, we want some of your jobs. And we want to bring into your safe, comfortable environment somebody that's going to make life a little bit more difficult for you on a day-to-day basis — because you won't be able to make assumptions about the music you're going to play in the office, the places you will go on retreats. This new employee might not want to do those things. And now you have to hear why." It adds many more complications to the office culture equations that these companies have never had to consider. I recognize that's a very heavy lift.

In many ways, that's a tension we see throughout corporate America. As I mentioned before, the television show *Black-ish* brilliantly mines this territory. That's the basic joke underlying the show, what happens when you bring black people into these white spaces. I've dealt with that question throughout my career, though my experiences haven't been quite so hilarious. I confronted it as a young attorney working at a white firm in New Jersey and certainly continue to confront it in the environmental world. But I have to refrain from being too critical of these white companies because I understand. After all, when I look out at the GYF staff, we are very close to 100 percent black, which was a conscious decision we made because we wanted to have a staff that looked like us. We wanted an office environment that was as comfortable for us as possible because of the challenging work we all face on a daily basis.

When companies bring us into their spaces and commit faux pas because they just don't know, do we give them a pass? We confronted this issue head-on and started training both our students who would be going into these white environments and the predominantly white organizations and agencies. If we place young people somewhere and they have a horrible experience and leave with a bitter taste, it will quickly undermine all of our efforts. No one will want to work at these sites. We talk to the young people about what they will face there, to prepare their expectations. We tell them about the social situations they will be encountering, how to respond when they're being asked to spend time after work with their colleagues and supervisors and they don't want to. And what the music and food will be like. In fact, I remember having a long conversation with a new intern about the types of food they might encounter at the company's cafeteria like kale and quinoa. And things they can do on their days off. We decided to employ a buddy system for many of the sites, after we learned how isolating and difficult it can be for one intern at some remote site in a part of the country where there weren't many people who looked like them. It's so much easier for them if they are there with a partner. We learned from a couple of bad experiences, in places like Wyoming and Tennessee. During a tour that one of the interns was giving at a site in Tennessee, while he was doing his interpretive work a little white girl said something to him that was racially derogatory and painful. At one site, our interns were living in substandard living quarters that were different than everybody else's, a place with bed bugs and all sorts of other unpleasant things that weren't even up to code. It was so upsetting when they told us what they were being subjected to. We were asking these young people to go to some remote location, likely with no Wi-Fi, no car, no place where they can get videos to rent, nothing. In effect, we're asking 20-year-olds to be trailblazers, to be the first persons of color to work in some of these places. Now when we interview kids, I sometimes feel like we're trying to find a bunch of Jackie Robinsons, looking for someone who will be strong enough to withstand whatever will be thrown at them. During the interviews, we purposely try to shake them up by presenting them with different situations they might face, asking how they will respond. If their answers aren't satisfactory, we know we're going to be sending them to an easier site like Tuskegee or MLK, where they will face very little to no racial tension.

What we're talking about here is quality of life, something these federal agencies definitely need to consider when they're considering bringing in people of color to do this work. The Park Service expects its employees to be flexible, to be open to moving around to different sites. But when the employees are moving, there needs to be some consideration given to their quality of life. Where will they get their hair done? Is there anywhere for them to socialize, to have fun outside of work? If they don't have answers to these questions, we know our young people are going to have a difficult time there. I know it's an issue with which these agencies are struggling, especially as they look at the coming silver tsunami of retirements among their workforce. How do they diversify public lands in areas that are extremely homogeneous? It's a real challenge. We told the Park Service that we all needed to do more to prepare these sites for our young people. We said, "We're doing our part in preparing these students, but somebody needs to talk to these supervisors because they're on the front line with them, they're the direct supervisors. They're the ones that are providing feedback and making these experiences not positive for them. So it's undoing all this work because the students then run, they never want to experience it again, and they tell 10 people on their way out."

We decided that we need to be doing webinars for the supervisors, while the Park Service does its own cultural sensitivity training. It's no longer acceptable for these sites to say, "Oh, well we didn't know. This was our first time." Were you living in a bubble?

During the webinars, we walk them through situations they might face in interacting with our young people, issues like entertainment, socialization. We try to address all the different pain points they might encounter. Earlier I told the story of the park ranger in the mountains of California connecting with an all-black youth corps by demonstrating that he knew their dances. That opened up a door for a relationship. He now uses that story in doing cultural sensitivity training, about the importance of finding connections. Of course, my advice isn't that all white people need to learn how to do hip-hop dancing to connect to black kids. But I *would* suggest that they make the effort to understand the kids, to know what interests them, what makes them tick. There might be unexplored areas of common interest that you otherwise wouldn't have known about. The point is that you need to be intentional about it. This isn't going to happen by accident, by osmosis. It's a point that resonates across corporate America, as we all are increasingly working with people who may not look like us. You can't assume everyone wants to do the same things, go to the same places. When I worked with the Trust for Public Land, I discovered that I was expected to socialize in the hot tub on our retreats. I was like, *Ewww, I'm not cool with grabbing a beer and getting into a hot tub with my co-workers.* That's a no-go for me. When we all went to the retreat in Sonoma County, there was so much taken for granted about what we would be doing together. They hadn't given it much thought. It all was seen as some type of reward, but it wasn't pleasurable for me. And I'm a well-educated, middle-class black woman who has spent decades in their world. I can't even imagine how challenging it must be for an 18-year-old in many of these situations.

I can vividly recall my experiences early in my career being thrust into predominantly white environments and colliding with the culture clash. At the mid-sized boutique law firm where I worked in New Jersey, I was the poster child for diversity. Any time there was a case or situation where they would benefit from having a brown face in the vicinity, I'd get called in. If there was a picture to be taken, my phone would ring, even if my department had nothing to do with it. The same thing happened when I joined the foundation world. I would feel uncomfortable at the holiday parties, but we wouldn't be allowed to bring our spouses — to be honest, probably because of all the office affairs going on between the attorneys and the staff. The firm culture was very white and very male, not exactly an optimal environment for a 30-year-old black woman. I had a hard time envisioning a future there. I had no mentors, nobody I felt any connection to, even though I tried reaching out to some of the women. When it becomes apparent to you that the culture is very different from your own, it takes a great deal of confidence to think that you can take on the culture by yourself and change it. Not many people in the early stages of their career have the self-assurance to do that — to change a culture that might have been decades in the making. I try to keep this reality front of mind when thinking about sending GYF interns into cultures that might be resistant to change. It's a wonderful thing to push these spaces to open themselves up to more diversity, but that can't be where the story ends. It is incumbent upon all parties to think about the environment the young people are stepping into and make sure it is as welcoming as possible. I have a good friend with whom I've been having deep conversations about these same issues in the field of technology. Kamau Bobb is a national authority in STEM education who is a former Program Officer at the National Science Foundation (NSF) and the founding Senior Director of the Constellations Center for Equity in Computing at Georgia Tech. He's been grappling with the culture changes that need to happen in the tech world to make it somewhat welcoming to young people of color, understanding that getting us in the door is only a small part of the struggle. If the young people are miserable after they get in the door, we're not doing anybody any favors. What winds up happening is we see far too much painful attrition — people of color fleeing to find more amenable cultures. If they leave, depriving the field of their diversity of thought and innovation, the results will be disastrous. Real progress will be elusive.

I should add here that culture shock is about more than skin color. We've had some incidents at GYF that demonstrated to me how much we need to expand our minds when it comes to this issue. I learned the mistake of making assumptions about my staff just because we all happen to be black. I have gotten more into wellness and stress relief over the years, especially after my health challenges I talked about earlier. I decided we would do a whole "stress relief" day at GYF, where I would bring in someone to lead us in yoga, somebody else to do meditation. I was excited to introduce the young adults to some of these stress-relieving techniques I have come to rely on heavily over the years. After we got going, I was surprised when one of them objected.

"I really don't feel comfortable," he said. It turns out that he had been going through some difficulties in his personal life, and he was not in a space where he wanted to be alone with his thoughts. I had not considered anything like that. I'm constantly growing as I deal with my staff. But these are important moments, demonstrating the value of diversity and being considerate of many different viewpoints.

Diversity pushes us all to be more empathetic. And just as importantly, to be flexible. I'm reminded of the early days of GYF, when I would go into meetings with Ruth Kitchen, the white woman with whom I started the organization. She would sometimes notice when the person we were meeting with would direct most of their comments at her instead of me, even though I was the CEO. Sometimes they wouldn't look at me at all, assuming all along that Ruth must be the boss. Even after learning that I was the boss, they'd keep looking at her. She would sometimes say to me, "That's alright, I'll be your white woman." She meant that she was fine with providing them the cover they needed to be comfortable with us. That's why I love her to death — she completely got it.

My family actually has a history with this sort of bait and switch. When my parents opened a record and book store in downtown Jersey City in the late-1960s, they were the first black business owners along the major commercial strip on Newark Avenue. But they knew there were many people in the area who weren't ready to see black store owners. So they hired a white man to work behind the counter, leading most of the customers to assume he owned the business. After a couple of years of this necessary deception, they stepped out front and made it clear that the store was their business. I should add that they did get their share of ugly racial incidents, but they didn't let it deter them. Similarly, there were times when I couldn't let our meetings go down like that. Sometimes I would tell Ruth that I needed to step to the forefront for a particular meeting. In fact, on a few occasions, we decided she wouldn't even attend so that everyone would be forced to address me. It was important to me to demonstrate in some of these meetings that all of their assumptions about who would be leading an environmental organization need to be altered.

In the environmental sphere, as well as the rest of the business world, we have no choice as a country but to open up these cultures to make them amenable and accessible to as many different types of people as possible. We've all read the stats about what American society will look like in coming years, how people of color will become the majority. If we don't figure out how to turn this thing around, the nation's future will be a dark, bleak landscape, our ignorance and stubbornness blocking out the much-needed light that just might save us all.

CHAPTER 8

Culturally Relevant Curriculum

IF YOU'RE GOING TO BRING environmental literacy to children of color, you have to employ a curriculum that resonates with communities of color. As I pointed out in chapter 1, we learned that lesson the hard way when we brought our curriculum to schools in Atlanta and had black kids looking at us like we were speaking Greek. You might have wonderful lessons and materials about watersheds and composting, but if you're not engaging the group of kids right in front of you, then it's all lost. A huge waste of time.

Schools have to make this a priority. The way kids are introduced to this information will affect their perspective on the environment for the rest of their lives. We have been extremely intentional in recent years to make sure we are trying to connect with our young people in every way possible, down to the tiniest detail.

First of all, you must have staff who look like the young people you are engaging. There's just no way around that one. It makes all the difference. If I'm a young person and I see someone who looks like me doing something that perhaps I want to do, a light bulb will pop on in my head. The realm of the possible is blown open. Maybe his hair is in locks, just like mine. Maybe her nails are colorfully painted like mine. Maybe he listens to the same music as I do.

This is something too many environmental groups have avoided for too long. They need one of those come-to-Jesus moments where they look inwardly and ask whether they're doing everything they can to engage diverse populations. Perhaps they're not 100 percent comfortable having others around them who don't look like them. When they say they want to reach these diverse audiences, how far are they willing to go?

The following is a lesson we have used over the years working with young people from diverse populations. It can serve as your template for how you should be thinking about this work.

Breath of Life

Topic: Air pollution and its effects

Goals:

+ Discover what causes air pollution
+ Analyze health effects
+ Determine action humans can take to improve air quality

Concepts:

+ Air pollution is the result of human and natural systems
+ Poor air quality directly impacts the health of living things
+ We all have the power to initiate changes in our daily lives

Skills:

+ Determining cause and effect
+ Analyzing
+ Observing

Materials:

+ Air Quality Index Poster and copies for each student
+ Smoker
+ Pictures of healthy and unhealthy lungs
+ Air Pollution Fact Board
+ Health Effects Fact Board
+ Materials for Car Count, Sample Collection, Smog Soup, or Acids Eating My Nose based on choice selection (See CLEAN 6)
+ 10 Things I Can Do to Keep the Air Clean on cardboard sheets
+ Parent letter

CLEAN 1: Kevin's Story

Using props (pictures of healthy and unhealthy lungs, inhaler, basketball, two big hands), the teacher reads or acts out Kevin's plight of dealing with the poor air quality in the city which exasperates his asthma condition.

Kevin is the best athlete in his fifth-grade class at P.S. 59. Basketball is his favorite sport, but he also likes football and soccer. Kevin can hardly get through his homework fast enough on most afternoons after school so that he can go outside and shoot hoops with his friends. His mother won't let him go to the park across the street from their apartment until he finishes his homework. But there are also other times when he must stay inside. When there is a lot of pollution in the city air, Kevin has to stay in the apartment so that he won't have asthma attacks. When he gets those, it feels like two big hands are wrapped around his neck, squeezing out the air so that Kevin can't breathe. Sometimes when he plays too long in polluted air, his breathing gets so bad the next day that he can't even go to school. Kevin has to take medicine through an inhaler when it gets really bad. Sometimes he even goes to the nurse's office for his treatment. Some weeks his mother can't afford to buy him more medicine. The medicine is very expensive. It's easier just to make him stay inside.

Discussion:

+ Why is there more pollution in the city?
+ What is asthma?
+ Why is asthma on the rise?
+ What are other consequences from air pollution?
+ What can we do to improve our air quality?

CLEAN 2: Air Pollution

Air Pollution Fact Board presented by teacher using pictures and a smoker.

Smog and particles in the air: Smog, otherwise known as ozone, is gas that you can't see or smell and can hurt the lungs. These pollutants come from our vehicle emissions and industrial and utility plants. Particle matter also comes from agricultural/farming practices such as burning fields or preparing the soil for planting. Sunlight and warm temperatures drive NOx (nitrogen oxides) and VOCs (volatile organic compounds) to react to form ozone. That is why we see more ozone in the summer, especially in the afternoons and early evenings.

CLEAN 3: Gaseous Charades

Teacher prepares cards with the following everyday occurrences that cause air pollution. Nine students are selected and given a card to act out to the class. The class as a whole or groups of students guesses what is being acted out.

+ Cars
+ Planes
+ Smoking
+ Chemicals: cleaners, paints, pesticides
+ Fires
+ Burning trash
+ Smoke from factories
+ Wasting electricity
+ Acid rain
+ Volcanoes

In the case of Kevin, why do you think there is more air pollution in the city?

CLEAN 4: Health Effects

Health Effects Fact Board presented by the teacher, referring back to how Kevin must feel. Highlight some of the fast facts and social and economic costs in a manner that is not threatening and at the students' level of understanding.

Immediate:
+ Wheezing
+ Irritated eyes
+ Sore throat
+ Feeling tired

- Shortness of breath
- Headache
- Cough
- Tightness in the chest

Long-term:
- Irritated airways
- More colds and infections

Asthma Overview
(Asthma and Allergy Foundation of America, aafa.org)

Asthma is characterized by inflammation of the air passages resulting in the temporary narrowing of the airways that transport air from the nose and mouth to the lungs. Asthma symptoms can be caused by allergens or irritants that are inhaled into the lungs, resulting in inflamed, clogged, and constricted airways. Symptoms include difficulty breathing, wheezing, coughing, and tightness in the chest. In severe cases, asthma can be deadly.

- There is no cure for asthma, but asthma can be managed with proper prevention and treatment.
- Asthma has a genetic component. If only one parent has asthma, chances are 1 in 3 that each child will have asthma. If both parents have asthma, it is much more likely (7 in 10) that their children will have asthma.
- More Americans than ever before say they are suffering from asthma. It is one of this country's most common and costly diseases.

Fast Facts: Asthma in America

Annual statistics on asthma in America:
- 26.5 million people have asthma.
- Asthma prevalence is higher in children (9.4 percent) than in adults (7.7 percent), and higher in females (9.2 percent) than males (7.0 percent).
- 1.7 million people visit the emergency room due to asthma.

+ 439,000 people are admitted to the hospital due to asthma.
+ 3,500 people die from asthma.
+ Asthma is the most common chronic illness in childhood, accounting for 13.8 million missed school days each year. It also accounts for 14.2 million lost work days for adults.
+ Asthma is slightly more prevalent among African Americans than Caucasians.
+ Ethnic differences in asthma prevalence, morbidity, and mortality are highly correlated with poverty, urban air quality, indoor allergens, lack of patient education, and inadequate medical care.

Economic Costs

The annual cost of asthma is estimated to be nearly $56 billion.

Images

Show pictures of healthy and unhealthy lungs.

CLEAN 5: Air Quality Index

The teacher will present the air quality index and explain the categories. Various scenarios will be reviewed and discussed.

+ Index value is 120: How should Kevin go about his day?
+ Index value is 70: How should Kevin go about his day?
+ People with lung disease, such as asthma, should reduce prolonged or heavy exertion outdoors at what levels?
+ The index indicates a level of 363: What should all of us do?

Have the students create their own scenarios and pose to the group for discussion.

CLEAN 6: Possible Activities: Car Count, Sample Collection, Smog Soup, or Acids Eating My Nose

Car Count

Take students out to a spot where they can observe traffic. Separate students into groups and for approximately 10 minutes count all cars with a single occupant. Record results and discuss ways in which we could reduce the number of cars on the road. Students go to the faculty parking lot and record the number of cars parked. Discuss ways in which the school employees can reduce the number of cars parked. Work in groups to prepare a poster or skit that can be presented to the administration.

Sample Collection

Collect samples of air pollution by placing Vaseline on either microscope slides or plastic sheet cut the size of a slide and place in different locations around the school. Check slides periodically and record results.

Smog Soup: Clean Air Campaign, A Recipe for Your Class

Smog is a word used to describe air pollution. Smog is created from chemical reactions created by gases reacting with heat and sunlight as well as solid and liquid masses released into the air. Smog is made up of volatile organic compounds (VOCs), nitrogen oxides (NOx), and particle pollution from sources including vehicle exhaust, diesel emissions, power plant emissions, vegetation, paints and solvents, dust and pollen, outdoor burning, and off-road mobile sources including tractors and other agriculture equipment. It is difficult to understand how all of these work together to create smog, so show your students how to create their own smog, and they will learn how it is formed!

What you need:

+ toy cars, trucks, tractors
+ paint brush
+ light bulb
+ picture of forest fire
+ picture of power plant
+ large soup pot
+ wooden spoon labeled with "heat" and "sun" sign
+ other representations of pollution sources/causes

Have students put everything in the pot one by one, explaining how they contribute to air pollution. Finally, mix together with the "sun" spoon (gently now, you do have a light bulb in there!) and explain that soup cannot be made without stirring together the ingredients — emphasizing the importance heat and sunlight play in creating smog. The more ingredients you have in the pot, the more smog you have in the air. Initiate a discussion on how some of those ingredients could be "pulled out" of the pot — how can we put fewer cars on the road, for example, and so on.

Acids Eating My Nose
(Hamilton County Department of Environmental Services Background)

Acid rain is more acidic than normal rain and forms through a complex process of chemical reactions involving air pollution. The two most important pollutants that contribute to acid rain are sulfur dioxide and nitrogen oxides, which react with moisture in the atmosphere to form acid rain. The sulfur and nitrogen compounds primarily come from human sources, such as automobiles, industries, and utilities. Acid rain can have many disguises. It can fall as snow, hail, sleet, or fog; it can even fall as dry particles. The true name for acid rain is really *acid deposition*, and can be classed as wet deposition (rain, sleet, etc.) or as dry deposition.

Acid rain can harm forests and crops by washing away nutrients and poisoning the plants. Bodies of water can have their pH altered so much that the aquatic life dies, or different, more acid tolerant, species take over. The corners of buildings can slowly be eaten away, and statues can be smoothed as ears, noses, and any other parts that stick out are slowly dissolved.

Don't panic! Acid rain is not a strong enough acid to harm you as it lands on your skin. Acid rain usually has a pH of about 5.4–5.6. Remember pure water has a pH of 1. If we compare acid rain to other everyday items, we can see that it is not as acidic as a lemon (pH 2.2) or even an apple (pH 3.0).

Purpose: To demonstrate the effect of acid rain on statues and buildings.

Objective: Students will learn how acid rain is an air pollution problem.

Materials:
+ Clear cups, glasses, or jars
+ Chalk
+ Vinegar
+ Optional: Long nails and a hammer

Time: 1 hour

Procedure:

1. Explain that acids react chemically with limestone.
2. Explain that vinegar is an acid and that chalk is limestone, or give your students pH paper and get them to assess whether vinegar is an acid or base.
3. Give each group a piece of chalk, and you can choose to give them a long nail to scratch a design in the side of the chalk. I usually go with squiggly lines or the students' initials. This will make their chalk unique, and will represent their statue.
4. Add vinegar to the group's glass/cup/jar and ask them to drop in their statue, observing closely.
5. Ask students about their observations.
6. Ask students what would happen if they had used acid rain instead of vinegar. You may want to remind them at this point that vinegar is more acidic than acid rain.
7. Ask the students if they should be concerned about acid rain? Why? How can we try and prevent it? (Remember the sources, factories, automobiles, and utilities)

Answers should relate to driving less (carpool, bus, bike, walk), saving energy (turning off lights, lowering AC), and buying less stuff (the 3 Rs: reduce, reuse, recycle).

CLEAN 7: Things we can do to help Kevin and keep the air clean

Have students record each of the ideas on a cardboard piece. Select 10 students and have them (with expression and movement) announce their idea to the group.

+ Plant a tree
+ Recycle
+ Ride a bike
+ Walk
+ Take a bus

+ Carpool
+ Don't waste electricity
+ Don't use spray products
+ Use fuel efficient cars
+ No idling

CLEAN 8: Clean Air Music

Breathe, breathe
In and out
Taking in clean air
Through the nose
To fill the lung
And out the mouth
Exhale!
(melody: "Row, Row, Row Your Boat")

CLEAN 9: Review

CLEAN 10: Dismissal

Take home a copy of the Air Quality Index and parent letter.

Parent Letter

This is intended to be the body of a hypothetical letter that a student might write to her/his parent about a classmate with asthma and the impact of air pollution on his asthma.

Living Energetically: Breath of Life

Wow! Kevin shared with us his health issues caused by poor air quality. Due to his asthma, he frequently has to stay inside on orange index days. He informed us of what everyday occurrences are causing air pollution and what kinds of health effects are impacting many all around us. Knowing how to find and interpret an Air Quality Index will help me evaluate the air quality conditions on a daily basis. I always thought our teacher was just being mean when saying we couldn't have recess outside on a beautiful sunny day. It is important that we help Kevin and all living things by reducing the amount of pollutants added to the air each day. I know our family can play a part in this by riding bikes more, recycling, carpooling, or maybe even planting a tree.

Appendix 1

Environmental Organizations Led by People of Color

N OT ALL ORGANIZATIONS are strictly environmental in approach, but may also include related issues, such as community sustainability and environmental justice.

A few organizations are included multiple times in different sections to represent different office locations. They generally work exclusively in these areas, whereas other multi-state orgs are working where they currently have projects, but are open to new locations. These latter ones are listed under the state where their home address is. Please forgive any mistakes. Reach out if your organization has been improperly placed, as some were not as obvious as others. The list was organized by state so that people can skip straight to one and see what orgs are there.

The database is far from complete. We will include an actively maintained version on our website. Stay tuned for updates!

States not included in the database means no organizations were found at the time. However, that does not mean none exist there.

Alabama

Federation of Southern Cooperatives Land Assistance Fund
Website: http://www.federationsoutherncoop.com/
Dedicated to assisting in land retention and development, especially for African Americans, but essentially for all family farmers. Programs include small farm and sustainable agriculture, land assistance, community-based forestry, cooperative marketing, and credit unions.

Contact (Rural Training & Research Center, Epes): fscepes@
federation.coop; (205) 652-9676

Alaska

Gwich'in Steering Committee

Website: http://ourarcticrefuge.org/
The Gwich'in Steering Committee is an organization that protects
Native rights and lands in Fairbanks, Alaska, especially against the oil
and gas industries. Active since 1988, they have consistently stood up
to oil drilling attempts that would disrupt the land and the animals
that live there, and destroy the people's way of life.
Contact: (907) 458-8264

Arizona

Black Mesa Water Coalition (BMWC Primary Location)

Website: https://www.blackmesawatercoalition.org/
BMWC works to organize Navajo and Hopi communities for the
protection of their lands, water, and youth, and thus serve as an environmental justice organization meant to provide a collective voice to
smaller communities, strengthening their approach. In addition to their
program that focuses on environmental justice and alternative energy
methods, they have a "restorative economy" program that focuses on
strengthening the culture and balancing how people relate to the natural world and a leadership development and movement program that
helps youth develop the skills needed to become leaders within their
own communities and connects BMWC with larger movements to
build the power of their work and the Indigenous communities.
Contact: contact@blackmesawatercoalition.org or blackmesawc@
gmail.com; (928) 213-5909

128

California

Asian Pacific Environmental Network (APEN)

Website: https://apen4ej.org/

APEN is an environmental justice organization focusing on bri... .g a collective voice to and educating the Asian and Pacific Islander communities on environmental, social, and economic issues. They work through creating movements and campaigns within the Oakland and Richmond areas, developing new leadership that will address issues within their communities, creating policy frameworks in response to ever-changing climate and economic divides, and engaging voters through proper issue education, as well as assisting with voter registration.

Contact: info@apen4ej.org; (510) 834-8920 (Oakland Main Office); (510) 236-4616 (Richmond Office)

California Indian Environmental Association

Website: http://www.ciea-health.org/

This environmental organization educates Indian communities about subsistence fishing, avoiding mercury and PCB in fish, and teaches environmental advocacy to youth. It seeks to empower communities to advocate for a cleaner California and become environmental stewards.

Contact: sherri@cieaweb.org

Central California Environmental Justice Network

Website: https://ccejn.org/

This organization works with small, poor, and generally voiceless communities throughout the San Joaquin Valley to educate them on environmental practices that will serve to improve their communities, provide technical assistance and resources to help them advocate for themselves, encourage youth to participate in environmental issues, and minimize environmental degradation within their communities.

Contact: nayamin.martinez@ccejn.org (Fresno County); gustavo. aguirrejr@ccejn.org (Kern County)

Communities for a Better Environment (CBE)

Website: http://www.cbecal.org/

CBE works to build the power of people living in California's communities of color and low-income communities in order to achieve environmental health and justice. They plan to do this by preventing and reducing pollution and building green, healthy, and sustainable communities and environments. CBE focuses on a variety of environmental issues, such as climate justice, clean energy, and green economy, as well as providing research on issues, litigating for change, and organizing campaigns.

Contact: (323) 826-9771 Huntington Park; (323) 826-9771 Wilmington; (323) 826-9771 East Oakland; (510) 302-0430 Richmond

Cultural Conservancy

Website: http://www.nativeland.org/

This Native-led nonprofit is dedicated to the preservation of Native culture, land, and rights. They have worked with a wide variety of Indigenous groups across the US, Canada, Pacific Islands, and South America on issues including environmental justice, sacred site protection and conservation, and revitalization of endangered languages and songs.

Contact: tcc@nativeland.org

Environmental Health Coalition

Website: https://www.environmentalhealth.org/index.php/en/

This environmental justice organization works locally within the San Diego and Tijuana region, as well as at a national and international level. They focus on reducing pollution and improving the health of low-income communities and communities of color.

Contact: frontdesk@environmentalhealth.org

Greenaction for Health and Environmental Justice
Website: http://greenaction.org/
Founded in 1997, this grassroots community organization works with low-income and working-class urban, rural, and Indigenous communities to fight for environmental justice and health.
Contact: greenaction@greenaction.org

People Organizing to Demand Environmental
and Economic Rights (PODER)
Website: https://www.podersf.org/
This organization focuses on empowering Latino immigrant families and low-income communities of color to create community solutions that lead to a society that prioritizes immigrant rights and social, racial, economic, and environmental justice. It works in several different locations and has partnered with other grassroots organizations to create programs in addition to their own.
Contact: info@podersf.org

Florida

Mahogany Youth Corporation (MYC)
Website: http://mahoganyyouth.com/index.html
MYC empowers youth by connecting them with nature through a STEM-based program, using fishing as a method of getting them interested. Through fishing, they discover more about nature and themselves, and see the components of the STEM program brought to life. MYC hopes that, through this program, youth will become more interested in marine biology and science.
Contact: info@mahoganyyouth.com; (305) 603-7451

Georgia

Federation of Southern Cooperatives Land Assistance Fund
Website: http://www.federationsoutherncoop.com/
This is dedicated to assisting in land retention and development, especially for African Americans but essentially for all family farmers.

Programs include small farm and sustainable agriculture, land assistance, community-based forestry, cooperative marketing, and credit unions.
Contact: info@federation.coop, (404) 765-0991 (Admin Office, East Point); fscalbany@federation.coop, (229) 432-5799 (Field Office, Albany)

HABESHA, Inc.

Website: http://habeshainc.org/
This organization works with African American youth and promotes principles and values emphasizing African culture and heritage, leadership, and environmental sustainability. Their various programs cultivate leadership skills; offer interactive learning of mathematics, science, nutrition, and environmental sustainability; and provide green job training in urban agriculture and agro-business development.
Contact: info@habeshainc.org; 1-888-308-7473

Proctor Creek Stewardship Council (PCSC)

Website: http://www.proctorcreek.org/
This organization in Atlanta spreads environmental awareness and stewardship to the communities within the Proctor Creek Watershed. They work with community members and organizations, as well as state and federal government, to clean up and survey the health of Proctor Creek and improve the quality of life of people living near or using the creek.
Contact: nojelks@wawa-online.org or freetheland@live.com

Truly Living Well

Website: https://www.trulylivingwell.com/
An urban agriculture farm that seeks to build a sustainable, dedicated local food economy in Metro Atlanta. They also have several programs dedicated to training adults and youth in urban agriculture, gardening basics, and maintaining a garden.
Contact: info@trulylivingwell.com; (678) 973-0997

West Atlanta Watershed Alliance (WAWA)

Website: http://wawa-online.org/

WAWA works to increase environmental stewardship and spread awareness of environmental issues within the communities of West Atlanta, while protecting green spaces and water quality. They have been working in West Atlanta since 1995, and are constantly getting involved and partnering with new organizations to create a cleaner, more sustainable West Atlanta.

Contact: info@wawa-online.org; (404) 752-5385

Hawaii

Ka Ohana O Kahikinui

Website: https://kahikinui.org/

An organization that works on the *moku* (district) of Kahikinui, Maui, to serve several purposes, all designed to maintain and improve the community for area families, including sustaining a land and natural resources management system, registering and restoring historical and archeological sites, and developing self-sufficiency through subsistence homesteading. They also work to create an economic hub in Hale Pili, and contributing to the Kahikinui Project, created by a Hawaiian group on the island of Maui that seeks to remove 500,000 pounds of wild organic protein.

Contact: info@kahikinui.org

The Kahikinui Project

Website: https://www.thekahikinuiproject.com/

The Kahikinui Project is actually the second phase of the restoration project, which is the removal of nearly 2,000 invasive ungulates within the conservation area. It also hopes to connect people to the story of the tiny Hawaiian community, who took the stewardship of their resources into their own hands and who — through their dedication, collectiveness, and love for the land — were able to bring back a forest, a forest that, in their own words, will serve as "a source of wonder and *aloha aina* into perpetuity."

Contact: jakemuise@gmail.com

Kūlaniākea

Website: https://www.kulaniakea.org/

Kūlaniākea is an organization that nurtures the spiritual, cultural, intellectual, social, emotional, and ethical development of children. They deliver a program of challenging academics, a strong sense of cultural identity through Hawaiian language and practice, critical thinking, accountability, global citizenship, and a cultivated relationship with the natural environment.

Contact: info@kulaniakea.org; (808) 247-3300

Kupu Hawaii

Website: http://www.kupuhawaii.org/

Kupu empowers youth to serve their community through character-building, service-learning, and environmental stewardship opportunities that encourage integrity with God, self, and others. Their hands-on training programs educate and mentor youth to become stewards of Hawaiian culture and environment and help them develop a strong connection to where they live.

Contact: info@kupuhawaii.org; (808) 735-1221

Illinois

Get Them to the Green

Website: http://www.getthemtothegreen.com/

An organization working in the South Side of Chicago to educate youth on environmental science and sustainability. They plan to work through three main programs: holding an annual week-long summer camp designed to foster an appreciation for environmental science in youth, creating and dispersing environmental science literature and teaching guides for Chicago public school teachers, and holding workshops in schools and community centers to create community gardens, aquaponics systems, and food science labs, all designed to increase understanding of sustainable systems and living. Other programs and events throughout the year continue engagement with youth and the community.

Little Village Environmental Justice Organization (LVEJO)

Website: http://www.lvejo.org/

This organization works to establish environmental justice for and achieve the self-determination of immigrant, lower-class, and working-class families in the Little Village community. Their accomplishments include helping shut down a coal plant whose toxicity infected many area residents, maintaining a bus route that many residents depended on, and fighting to get a Superfund dumping site remediated into usable green space. They continue to fight for and educate community members through internships, community events, volunteering opportunities, and toxic tours.

Contact: (773) 762-6991

People for Community Recovery (PCR)

Website: http://www.peopleforcommunityrecovery.org/

PCR is a community group that seeks to enhance the quality of life for communities affected by environmental pollution. They educate communities on environmental issues and advocate for policies to restore the environment, offer toxic tours of polluted areas, provide environmental career training, host development programs for résumés and interview skills, and advocate for housing rights.

Contact: info@peopleforcommunityrecovery.org; (773) 840-4618

Louisiana

Deep South Center for Environmental Justice (DSCEJ)

Website: http://www.dscej.org/

A central pillar of the environmental justice movement in the South, the DSCEJ works with many community organizations and HBCUs to serve as a great resource on environmental justice research and education. It also provides health and safety programs for environmental careers. In operation for over 20 years, it has numerous programs and connections for people, organizations, and colleges to review and collaborate with.

Contact: (504) 272-0956; (504) 372-3473 (fax)

Federation of Southern Cooperatives Land Assistance Fund

Website: http://www.federationsoutherncoop.com/

Dedicated to assisting in land retention and development, especially for African Americans but essentially for all family farmers, its programs include small farm and sustainable agriculture, land assistance, community-based forestry, cooperative marketing, and credit unions.

Contact: bruceharrell@federation.coop

Gulf Coast Center for Law & Policy

Website: https://www.gcclp.org/

The Gulf Coast Center is a public-interest law firm that works to promote ecological equality for communities of color in Louisiana. They have legal services for communities that need it, and host community events and informationals as well.

Contact: info@gcclp.org; (985) 643-6186

Launch NOLA Green

Website: https://www.urbanconservancy.org/launch-nola-green/

Launch NOLA Green is another initiative of Thrive New Orleans, which helps communities and small businesses thrive in their pursuits, and is designed to assist small businesses become leaders within the water economy. The program teaches participants how to incorporate water management into residential landscaping projects to combat flooding and subsidence.

Contact: (504) 717-6187

Lower 9th Ward Center for Sustainable Engagement and Development (CSED)

Website: http://sustainthenine.org/

The CSED focuses on coastal rehabilitation, greening the built environment, and increasing food security in New Orleans' Lower 9th Ward. Their goal is to help rebuild an equitable, sustainable, and resilient community, and they partner with organizations and projects to help

them reach this goal. They also have volunteer and assistance programs for residents to take advantage of.
Contact: info@sustainthenine.org; (504) 324-9955

Michigan

East Michigan Environmental Action Council (EMEAC)

Website: http://www.emeac.org/
EMEAC seeks to empower the Detroit community to protect, preserve, and value land, water, and air. They do this through community building programs, such as youth development training, environmental justice education, and collaborative relationship building. They have been working to address environmental issues and concerns in East Michigan since the 1960s.
Contact: (313) 556-1702

Minnesota

Indigenous Environmental Network

Website: http://www.ienearth.org/
This organization works to address environmental and economic justice issues through capacity building of Native communities and tribal governments in order to develop mechanisms that will protect their sacred sites, land, water, air, natural resources, health of both their people and all living things, and to build economically sustainable communities. They serve as an informational clearinghouse, organize campaigns and direct actions to increase public awareness, help develop initiatives that will impact policy, and build alliances among Indigenous communities and organizations, and other people-of-color organizations and communities. They hold local, regional, and national meetings on environmental and economic justice issues, and serve as a support, resource, and referral to Indigenous communities and youth throughout primarily North America, and in recent years, globally.
Contact: (218) 751-4967

Mississippi

Federation of Southern Cooperatives Land Assistance Fund
Website: http://www.federationsoutherncoop.com/
Dedicated to assisting in land retention and development, especially for African Americans but essentially for all family farmers, its programs include small farm and sustainable agriculture, land assistance, community-based forestry, cooperative marketing, and credit unions.
Contact: mscenter@mindspring.com; (601) 354-2750 (Field Office, Jackson)

New York

New York City Environmental Justice Alliance
Website: http://www.nyc-eja.org/
This citywide membership network links environmental companies to communities of color and low-income communities struggling with issues of environmental injustice. It helps facilitate contact between organizations and those in need of such services.
Contact: http://www.nyc-eja.org/contact/

UPROSE
Website: https://www.uprose.org/
This intergenerational women-of-color-led environmental organization promotes sustainability and resiliency in Brooklyn. They work through community organizing, Indigenous and youth leadership development, education, and cultural and artistic expression.
Contact: info@uprose.org; (718) 492-9307

We Act (Headquarters)
Website: https://www.weact.org/
This organization started in 1988 to combat environmental racism in West Harlem. It has grown to be a central and active environmental justice organization in New York City and Washington DC, serving to inform and empower low-income and communities of color on environmental issues and ideas relevant to them, and most importantly

encourage their participation in the creation of fair environmental protections and policies.

Contact: info@weact.org

North Carolina

Student Environmental Education Coalition

Website: https://www.ncseec.org/

This youth-run organization focuses on teaching environmental literacy to youth, promoting them to become future leaders in the environmental field.

Contact: contact@ncseec.org

Ohio

Environmental Health Watch (EHW)

Website: https://www.ehw.org/

EHW focuses on creating healthy homes and communities by engaging community members and removing environmental hazards from their homes. They also teach partners, community members, and other interested people environmental education and technical assistance.

Contact: (216) 961-4646

Oregon

Organizing People/Activating Leaders (OPAL)

Website: http://www.opalpdx.org/

OPAL seeks to cultivate leadership among people of low-income and communities of color. They partner with other organizations to create a vast network that has more access to communities in need, and provides them with the resources they need to pursue environmental health and equity. OPAL also creates campaigns for environmental issues, provides youth leadership training, and tackles transit justice.

Contact: info@opalpdx.org; (503) 774-4503

Pennsylvania

Soil Generation

Website: http://www.groundedinphilly.org/soil-generation-about/
This coalition of individuals, farmers, gardeners, and community organizations helps communities of color regain control of land and food. They provide access to resources that determine land use, growth of food, addressing health concerns, and improving the environment. They hold monthly community meetings.
Contact: http://www.groundedinphilly.org/contact/

Tennessee

Diving with a Purpose (DWP)

Website: http://www.divingwithapurpose.org/index.html
DWP focuses on conservation and protection of submerged heritage resources by providing adults and youth with training, education, certification, and field experience in maritime archaeology and ocean conservation. They particularly focus on the protection, documentation, and interpretation of African slave trade shipwrecks.
Contact: anything@divingwithapurpose.org; (615) 730-4906

Texas

Achieving Community Tasks Successfully (ACTS)

Website: https://acts-organization.org/
This community organization provides education and resources to the Historic Pleasantville community, which has traditionally not had access otherwise to such information. They focus on environmental justice in the broadest sense, and have an intergenerational focus to make sure information is passed on and the community becomes more active as a whole.
Contact: https://acts-organization.org/contacts/

Great Plains Restoration Council (GPRC)

Website: http://gprc.org/

GPRC is an ecological health organization that restores and protects native ecosystems, particularly damaged prairies, plains, and waters, for the purpose of improving the health of people and communities. They teach eco health practices and principles nationally, and uses media engagement and literary arts to expand community awareness and engagement.

Contact: (832) 598-GPRC (4772)

Southwest Workers Union

Website: https://www.swunion.org/

This community-serving organization fights for workers' rights, environmental justice, and increasing community presence in elections. They have represented their communities for over 30 years and have gained several victories and affected numerous policy changes for wage rights, environmental health and justice, fair redistricting lines, and more.

Contact: info@swunion.org; (210) 299-2666

Texas Environmental Justice Advocacy Services (t.e.j.a.s.)

Website: http://tejasbarrios.org/

This organization is dedicated to educating community members about health concerns caused by pollution and empowering them through advocating for their needs, as well as informing them of what actions they as a community can take to ensure they have a cleaner and healthier environment. They have several different advocacy campaigns, as well as offer community air monitoring services and toxic tours designed to help individuals and communities gain first-hand insight into environmental justice issues.

Contact: http://tejasbarrios.org/contact/

Washington

Front and Centered

Website: https://frontandcentered.org/

Front and Centered is an organization with the goal of creating jobs and improving the health of communities as we transition to a just, clean economy. This statewide coalition of 60 organizations and communities of low-income and color works to build partnerships, develop and advocate for policies, educate and mobilize voters, and work on communications and storytelling.

Contact: christina@frontandcentered.org

Got Green

Website: http://gotgreenseattle.org/

This environmental, racial, and economic justice organization is dedicated to teaching and growing community leaders to be voices within the Green Movement and is committed to making sure its benefits reach low-income and communities of color.

Contact: info@gotgreen.org

Washington DC

MobilizeGreen

Website: https://www.mobilizegreen.org/

MobilizeGreen provides internships, mentoring, and engagement for youth who wish to learn more about the environmental field and related careers. Through this method of outreach, they can address the lack of diverse leadership within nonprofit environmental organizations and government agencies.

Contact: (202) 375-7760

WE ACT

Website: https://www.weact.org/

This organization started in 1988 to combat environmental racism in West Harlem. It has grown to be a central and active environmental justice organization in New York City and Washington DC, and serves to inform and empower low-income and communities of color on environmental issues and ideas relevant to them, and most importantly encourage their participation in the creation of fair environmental protections and policies.

Contact: info@weact.org

Non-state Specific

Diné C.A.R.E.

Website: https://www.dine-care.org/

This Native American environmental group serves to empower and protect the interests of the Diné (Navajo) communities. They work across multiple environmental issues and reservations, and have a long and established history of fighting against environmental injustice and negligence. C.A.R.E. stands for Citizens Against Ruining our Environment.

Contact: dinecare88@gmail.com

Eastern Sierra Conservation Corps

Website: http://www.easternsierracc.org/

This developmental and leadership program provides participants with a unique opportunity to work within nature, discovering themselves and deepening their appreciation for the wilds. They specialize in populations generally underrepresented in National Park and Forest sites and expanding how our natural resources are understood and utilized.

Contact: info@easternsierracc.org

Green for All

Website: http://www.greenforall.org/

This organization is dedicated to giving a voice to people of color and working families in the climate movement. They advocate for environmental justice and host toolkits that focus on building a pathway to using green power for states. They work across states and can help connect green leaders in the fight to help right our ecosystem wrongdoings.

Contact: info@greenforall.org; (510) 663-6500

Greening Youth Foundation (GYF)

Website: https://www.gyfoundation.org/

GYF works with diverse, underserved, and underrepresented children, youth, and young adults in an effort to develop and nurture enthusiastic and responsible environmental stewards. GYF's cultural-based environmental education programing engages local children and exposes them to healthy lifestyle choices in order to create an overall healthy community. They also believe that youth and young adults from diverse backgrounds can greatly benefit from the career opportunities presented within the state and federal land management sectors. Accordingly, they continue to develop and strengthen partnerships with land management agencies to provide service and internship opportunities for youth and young adults, thereby creating pathways to careers in conservation, land management, and environmental service.

Contact: contact@gyfoundation.org; (404) 254-4827

GreenLatinos

Website: http://www.greenlatinos.org/

This national organization hosts conventions consisting of a broad coalition of Latino leaders who work to address national, local, and regional environmental, natural resource, and conservation issues affecting the Latino community across the US. They establish partnerships and networks, as well as develop and advocate for policies and programs that advance their mission. They host an annual Core Summit to establish their core policy priorities for that year.

Contact: See main page for contact form (must scroll down)

Hispanic Access Foundation (HAF)

Website: https://www.hispanicaccess.org/

HAF connects Latinos with partners and opportunities to improve their lives and create an equitable society. Through partnerships with faith and community organizations, they increase access to vital information and community resources for the Hispanic community. Their method of outreach and vast network of Hispanic-serving organizations allow them to coordinate projects and help people on a national level.

Contact: info@hispanicaccess.org; (202) 640-4342

Hispanic Heritage Foundation

Website: https://hispanicheritage.org/

Started by the White House in 1987, it promotes cultural pride and promise through public awareness campaigns, and hosts many training and learning workshops across the country, as well as provides internships and positions within nonprofits and government agencies.

Contact: info@hispanicheritage.org; (202) 558-9473

Inter-Tribal Environmental Council (ITEC)

Website: https://itec.cherokee.org/

ITEC serves to protect the health of Native Americans, their natural resources, and the environment as related to land, air, and water. It provides technical support, training, and environmental services to its member tribes in Oklahoma, New Mexico, and Texas.

Contact: karen-dye@cherokee.org; (918) 453-5109

Online Organization/Social Movement

Brown Environmentalist Media Co.

Website: https://been.media/brownenvironmentalist.org/

This online organization focuses on amplifying the media presence of the experiences, contributions, and leadership of black, Indigenous, and people of color in the environment.

Brown People Camping

Website: https://www.brownpeoplecamping.com/

This social media initiative uses digital storytelling and personal narrative to promote greater diversity in camping and exploring our public lands.

Diversify Outdoors

Website: https://www.diversifyoutdoors.com/

This social movement is dedicated to inspiring diversity within outdoor recreation and conservation.

Melanin Base Camp

Website: https://www.melaninbasecamp.com/

This social movement is similar to Diversify Outdoors but with a focus on outdoor adventure sports.

Native Womens Wilderness

Website: https://www.nativewomenswilderness.org/

This organization promotes and aspires to educate Native and Non-Natives on the heritage of the Ancestral and Public Lands of the country and raise the voices of Native women in the outdoor space. It also promotes representation of women of color in advertising of outdoor retailers, encourages exploration of nature, and emphasizes a healthy lifestyle within the wilderness.

POC/Diverse Outdoor/Eco Activities Groups

Black Freedom Outfitters

Website: http://www.blackfreedomoutfitters.com/

This organization provides outdoor adventures that highlight geographies of cultural, political, and social significance to black people, as well as environmental stewardship and leadership programs

The Black Outdoors

Website: https://www.theblackoutdoors.com/

This organization is dedicated to bringing diversity to the outdoors through events, storytelling, information about gear needed for certain activities, tips and tricks to make the best of your outdoor time, reviews, and recommendations on places to visit.

Brothers of Climbing Crew

Website: https://boccrew.com/

This organization, dedicated to bringing diversity into the rock-climbing space, works with other organizations to help create and promote events, such as Color the Crag.

The Brown Ascenders

FB page: https://www.facebook.com/thebrownascenders/

This organization of POC rock climbers hosts events in California.

Brown Girls Climb

Website: https://www.browngirlsclimb.com/

This organization is dedicated to promoting diversity in the climbing space, creating a community of color for climbers and leadership opportunities for females of color. It offers underrepresented communities inclusive opportunities to climb and explore. They hold meetings in Washington and Denver.

Flash Foxy

Website: http://flashfoxy.com/

This organization celebrates women climbing with women and serves as a place/online presence to inspire and connect. They host several climbing festivals in multiple locations, so check their website for a location near you.

Latino Outdoors

Website: http://latinooutdoors.org/

This organization has goals similar to Outdoor Afro but focuses on Latino Americans. It serves to give a stronger presence to the Latino voice in the outdoors and conservation movement, create more networking opportunities for Latinos working in conservation, and provide cultural connections to nature that other outdoor programs may overlook.

LatinXHikers

Website: https://www.latinxhikers.com/journal

This organization started as a social media platform to promote diversity in the outdoors through digital storytelling and has now evolved to host group and community hiking events.

Outdoor Afro

Website: http://outdoorafro.com/

This organization seeks to get minority groups, particularly African American, more involved with nature through organized meet-ups for hiking, kayaking, camping, and environmental education training. This serves to create a connection with their environment and inspire a willingness to protect nature, as well as provide healing, promote an activ

Outdoor Asian

Website: https://www.outdoorasian.com/about

This organization is dedicated to bringing more Asians and Pacific Islanders into the outdoors, hosting events and workshops to promote outdoor activities and change views about the environment and the role of nature within our lives. Local organizations are in Washington, Oregon, Colorado, and San Francisco Bay.

e, healthy lifestyle, and show how nature can connect to black history.

POC/Diverse Outdoor Equipment Stores

NativesOutdoors

Website: https://www.natives-outdoors.org/

An outdoor apparel store with products designed and made by Native Americans, with a portion of profits going to Native nonprofits working on outdoor recreation, language and culture revitalization, and environmental issues.

Other Databases on Environmental Organizations (Not Necessarily POC): General

Alabama

http://www.ag.auburn.edu/auxiliary/grassroots/
http://www.ag.auburn.edu/auxiliary/grassroots/inactive.php
http://www.voicesfromthevalley.org/organizations/

Connecticut

http://www.caccmi.org/useful-links/

Hawaii

http://www.greenlisthawaii.com/page7.html

POC Climate Justice and EJ

https://pocinecj.org/environmental-climate-justice-professionals/

Other Cool Stuff and Groups We've Come Across

https://www.racialequitytools.org/home
https://www.aglanta.org/
http://peoplestown.com/
https://anothergulf.com/
http://ceed.org/
https://projectjatropha.com/
https://detroitenvironmentaljustice.org/
https://www.eco-d.org/
https://www.facebook.com/SouEcho/
http://www.projecttgif.com/
https://www.casustentables.org/
http://www.broweryouthawards.org/awardees/
https://kokuahawaiifoundation.org/home
https://www.facebook.com/CanYouthDelegation/
https://www.sunrisemovement.org/
https://ecc-ucla.weebly.com/
https://www.stopline3.org/

https://www.facebook.com/utahyes/
http://www.broweryouthawards.org/awardees/
http://www.etctrips.org/about
http://brothersontherise.org/
http://www.yesfamilies.org/staff-board

Appendix 2

Historically Black Colleges and Universities (HBCUs)

A N ASTERISK (*) indicates that one or several environmental degrees are available under the school/program of study.

Note: Environmental degrees strictly focus on an environmental aspect. As such, degrees like agriculture, aquaculture, marine biology, and environmental science count, whereas chemistry and (ordinary) biology do not.

Alabama

Alabama A&M University (Normal, AL)

Founded in 1875, this public university has four colleges of study and a graduate school:

+ College of Agricultural, Life and Natural Sciences*
+ College of Business and Public Affairs
+ College of Education, Humanities and Behavioral Sciences
+ College of Engineering, Technology and Physical Sciences

Alabama State University (Montgomery, AL)

Founded in 1867, this public university has six colleges of study and a graduate school:

+ College of Business Administration
+ College of Education
+ College of Health Sciences
+ College of Liberal Arts & Social Sciences

- College of Science, Mathematics & Technology
- College of Visual & Performing Arts
- Division of Aerospace Studies
- Continuing Education

Bishop State Community College (Mobile, AL)

Founded in 1927, this public university has eight areas of study and a Technical/Workforce Development Program that has short- and long-term certificates, as well as an Associate Degree:

- Business & Economics
- Developmental Education
- Early Childhood Education
- Health-Related Professions
- Humanities
- Mathematics
- Natural Sciences
- Social Sciences

Gadsden State Community College (Gadsden, AL)

Founded in 1925, this public university has ten academic divisions of study, a dedicated Health Sciences Division, and a Technology & Engineering Division on Technical Skills and Jobs:

- Alabama Language Institute
- Division of Business, Legal Studies, and Computer Science
- Developmental Studies
- Fine Arts
- Health, PE, & Recreation Division
- Language and Humanities Division
- Math and Engineering Division
- Social Sciences Division
- Science Division
- Skills Training Division

J.F. Drake State Community & Technical College (Huntsville, AL)

Founded in 1961, this public college has four academic divisions of study:

+ Business, Computer Science, and Engineering Technologies
+ General and Developmental Education
+ Health Sciences Technologies
+ Applied Services Technologies

Lawson State Community College (Bessemer, AL)

Founded in 1949, this public college has four programs of study:

+ Business & Technologies
+ College Transfer (General Studies)
+ Career Technical Programs
+ Health Professions

Miles College (Fairfield, AL)

Founded in 1905, this private college, religiously affiliated with CME Church, has six colleges of study:

+ Business & Accounting
+ Communications
+ Education
+ Humanities
+ Social & Behavioral Sciences
+ Natural Sciences & Mathematics*

Oakwood University (Huntsville, AL)

Founded in 1896, this private university, religiously affiliated with Seventh-Day Adventist, has five colleges of study:

+ School of Arts & Sciences
+ School of Business & Information Systems
+ School of Education & Social Sciences
+ School of Nursing & Health Professions
+ School of Religion

Selma University (Selma, AL)

Founded in 1878, this is a private university, religiously affiliated with Alabama State Missionary Baptist Convention.

Shelton State Community College (Tuscaloosa, AL)

Founded in 1952, this public college has 8 areas of study, as well as offering 16 technical and 5 health programs:
+ Behavioral Science
+ Business/Computer Science
+ Fine Arts
+ Health, Wellness, Food, & Nutrition
+ Humanities & Communications Arts
+ Language
+ Mathematics
+ Natural Sciences

Stillman College (Tuscaloosa, AL)

Founded in 1876, this private college, religiously affiliated with the Presbyterian Church, has three schools, as well as a Theology Certificate program and accelerated business program for adults:
+ School of Arts & Sciences
+ School of Business
+ School of Education

Talladega College (Talladega County, AL)

Founded in 1867, this private college, religiously affiliated with United Church of Christ, has four divisions of study and a graduate school:
+ Division of Business and Administration
+ Division of Humanities and Fine Arts
+ Division of Natural Sciences and Mathematics
+ Division of Social Sciences and Education

Trenholm State Technical College (Montgomery, AL)

Founded in 1947, this public college has three divisions of study:
- Academic Division (a variety of degrees)
- Allied Health Division
- Career/Technical Education Division

Tuskegee University (Tuskegee, AL)

Founded in 1881, this private university has eight different colleges and schools, as well as a graduate school:
- College of Business and Information Science
- College of Agriculture, Environment, and Nutrition Science*
- College of Arts & Sciences
- College of Engineering
- College of Veterinary Medicine
- School of Agriculture and Construction Science
- School of Education
- School of Nursing and Allied Health

Arkansas

Arkansas Baptist College (Little Rock, AR)

Founded in 1884, this private college, religiously affiliated with the Baptist Church, has six academic departments of study:
- Business
- General Studies
- Public Administration
- Religious Studies
- Social and Behavioral Sciences

Philander Smith College (Little Rock, AR)

Founded in 1877, this private United Methodist university has seven academic departments of study:
- Division of Business Administration
- Division of Education
- Division of Arts and Humanities

+ Division of Social Sciences
+ Division of Natural and Physical Sciences
+ Continuing Education and Professional Studies
+ Dual Degree Programs

Shorter College (Little Rock, AR)

Founded in 1886, this private college, religiously affiliated with African Methodist Episcopal Church, offers five associate art degree programs:
+ General Studies
+ Church Leadership and Ministry
+ Childhood Development
+ Criminal Justice
+ Entrepreneurial Studies

University of Arkansas at Pine Bluff (Pine Bluff, AR)

Founded in 1873, this public university offers four schools of study and a graduate program:
+ School of Agriculture, Fisheries, and Human Sciences*
+ School of Arts & Sciences
+ School of Business and Management
+ School of Education

California

Charles R. Drew University of Medicine and Science (Los Angeles, CA)

Founded in 1966, this private university has three colleges of study:
+ College of Medicine
+ College of Science and Health
+ Mervyn M. Dymally School of Nursing

Delaware

Delaware State University (Dover, DE)

Founded in 1891, this public university has four colleges of study and a graduate school:
+ College of Agriculture, Science, and Technology*
+ College of Humanities, Education & Social Sciences
+ College of Business
+ College of Health & Behavioral Science

District of Columbia, Washington

Howard University

Founded in 1867, this private university offers 12 schools of study, including law, as well as graduate, doctorate, and professional programs:
+ Arts & Sciences*
+ Business
+ Communications
+ Dentistry
+ Divinity
+ Education
+ Engineering & Architecture
+ Law
+ Medicine
+ Nursing & Allied Health Sciences
+ Pharmacy
+ Social Work

University of the District of Columbia

Founded in 1851, this public university has four main academic colleges and offers a graduate program, School of Law, and Community College:
+ College of Agriculture, Urban Sustainability & Environmental Sciences*
+ College of Arts & Sciences
+ School of Business & Public Administration
+ School of Engineering and Applied Sciences

Florida

Bethune-Cookman University (Daytona Beach, FL)

Founded in 1904, this private university, religiously affiliated with the United Methodist Church, has nine schools of study and a master's program:

+ Business and Entrepreneurship.
+ Education
+ Health Sciences
+ Hospitality Management
+ Liberal Arts
+ Nursing
+ Performing Arts and Communication
+ Religion
+ Science, Engineering, and Mathematics*

Edward Waters College (Jacksonville, FL)

Founded in 1866, this private college, religiously affiliated with AME Church, has eight academic departments:

+ Biology
+ Business
+ Criminal Justice
+ Communications
+ Education
+ Mathematics
+ Music
+ Psychology

Florida A&M University (Tallahassee, FL)

Founded in 1887, this public university has 12 schools of study, a law school and offers master's, professional, and doctoral degrees:

+ College of Agriculture and Food Science*
+ College of Education
+ College of Engineering
+ College of Pharmacy and Pharmaceutical Sciences

- College of Social Sciences, Arts and Humanities
- College of Science and Technology
- School of Allied Health Science
- School of Architecture and Engineering Technology
- School of Business and Industry
- School of the Environment*
- School of Journalism and Graphic Communication
- School of Nursing

Florida Memorial University (Miami Gardens, FL)

Founded in 1879, this private university, religiously affiliated with American Baptist Churches USA, offers three schools of study and has a master's program:

- School of Arts and Sciences*
- School of Business
- School of Education

Georgia

Albany State University (Albany, GA)

Founded in 1903, this public university has five colleges of study and offers graduate degrees:

- College of Business
- College of Education
- College of Sciences & Technology
- College of Arts & Humanities
- Darton College of Health Professions

Clark Atlanta University (Atlanta, GA)

Founded in 1865, this private university, religiously affiliated with the United Methodist Church, has four schools of study and offers graduate degrees:

- School of Arts & Sciences
- School of Business
- School of Education
- School of Social Work

Fort Valley State University (Fort Valley, GA)

Founded in 1895, this public university has three colleges of study:
+ College of Arts & Sciences
+ College of Education and Professional Sciences
+ College of Agriculture, Family Sciences, and Technology*

Interdenominational Theological Center (Atlanta, GA)

Founded in 1958, this private institution operates as a professional graduate school of theology, offering the following degrees:
+ Master of Divinity
+ Master of Arts in Religion and Education
+ Doctor of Ministry

Morehouse School of Medicine (Atlanta, GA)

Founded in 1867, SoM in 1975, this private college offers three academics divisions of study:
+ Division of Business Administration & Economics
+ Division of Humanities & Social Sciences
+ Division of Science & Mathematics

The SoM offers 13 academic areas of study:

+ Community Health & Preventive Medicine
+ Family Medicine
+ Medical Education
+ Medicine
+ Microbiology, Biochemistry & Immunology
+ Neurobiology
+ Obstetrics & Gynecology
+ Pathology & Anatomy
+ Pediatrics
+ Pharmacology & Toxicology
+ Physiology
+ Psychiatry & Behavioral Sciences
+ Surgery

Paine College (Augusta, GA)

Founded in 1882, this private college, religiously affiliated with United Methodist Church and Christian Methodist Episcopal Church, has six academic departments of study:

+ Department of Humanities
+ Department of Mathematics, Sciences, and Technology
+ Department of Social Sciences
+ Department of Business
+ Department of Education
+ Department of Media Studies

Savannah State University (Savannah, GA)

Founded in 1890, this public university has four colleges of study:

+ College of Business Administration
+ College of Liberal Arts & Social Sciences
+ College of Science & Technology*
+ College of Education

Spelman College (Atlanta, GA)

Founded in 1881, this private college does not have traditional colleges but offers 34 majors, 36 minors, and more areas of study through its partnership with Clark Atlanta and Morehouse.

Kentucky

Kentucky State University (Frankfort, KY)

Founded in 1886, this public university has five colleges of study and a graduate program:

+ College of Agriculture, Communities, and the Environment*
+ College of Humanities and Social Sciences
+ College of Business and Computational Sciences
+ College of Natural, Applied, and Health Sciences
+ College of Public Service and Leadership Studies

Simmons College of Kentucky (Louisville, KY)

Founded in 1869, this private college has five bachelor of arts degrees and two associates of arts degrees:

+ BA in Business Entrepreneurship
+ BA in Cross-Cultural Communication
+ BA in Sociology
+ BA in Religious Studies
+ BA in Music
+ AA General Studies
+ AA Religious Studies

Louisiana

Dillard University (New Orleans, LA)

Founded in 1869, this private university, religiously affiliated with United Church of Christ and United Methodist Church, has three colleges of study:

+ College of Arts and Sciences
+ College of Nursing
+ College of Business

Grambling State University (Grambling, LA)

Founded in 1901, this public university has three colleges of study and a graduate school:

+ College of Arts and Sciences
+ College of Business
+ College of Education

Southern University and A&M College (Baton Rouge, LA)

Founded in 1880, this public university has six colleges of study and a graduate school:

+ College of Agricultural, Family and Consumer Sciences*
+ College of Business
+ Nelson Mandela College of Government and Social Sciences
+ College of Humanities and Interdisciplinary Studies

+ College of Nursing and Allied Health
+ College of Sciences and Engineering

Southern University at New Orleans (New Orleans, LA)

Founded in 1959, this public university has four colleges of study:

+ College of Arts & Sciences
+ College of Business Administration
+ College of Education and Human Development
+ School of Social Work

Southern University at Shreveport (Shreveport, LA)

Founded in 1967, this public university has three divisions of study that offer associate's degrees:

+ Division of Allied Health Sciences & Nursing
+ Division of Business, Science, Technology, Engineering, and Mathematics (BSTEM)
+ Division of Arts, Humanities, Social Sciences, and Education

Xavier University of Louisiana (New Orleans, LA)

Founded in 1915, this private university, religiously affiliated with the Roman Catholic Church, has two colleges of study and a graduate school:

+ College of Arts & Sciences
+ College of Pharmacy

Maryland

Bowie State University (Bowie, MD)

Founded in 1865, this public university has four colleges of study and a graduate school:

+ College of Arts & Sciences
+ College of Business
+ College of Education
+ College of Profession Studies

Coppin State University (Baltimore, MD)

Founded in 1900, this public university has four colleges of study and a graduate program:
+ College of Arts, Sciences, and Education
+ College of Behavioral & Social Sciences
+ College of Business
+ College of Health Professions

Morgan State University (Baltimore, MD)

Founded in 1867, this public university has nine colleges and schools of study and a graduate school:
+ College of Liberal Arts
+ School of Architecture & Planning
+ School of Business & Management
+ School of Community Health & Policy
+ School of Computer, Mathematic, and Natural Sciences
+ School of Education & Urban Studies
+ School of Engineering
+ School of Global Journalism & Communication
+ School of Social Work

University of Maryland Eastern Shore (Princess Anne, MD)

Founded in 1886, this public university has four departments of study and a graduate school:
+ School of Education, Social Sciences, and The Arts
+ School of Pharmacy and Health Professions
+ School of Business and Technology
+ School of Agricultural and Natural Sciences*

Mississippi

Alcorn State University (Lorman, MS)

Founded in 1871, this public university has five schools of study and a graduate school:
+ School of Agriculture and Applied Science*
+ School of Arts and Sciences
+ School of Business
+ School of Education and Psychology
+ School of Nursing

Coahoma Community College (Coahoma County, MS)

Founded in 1924, this public college has four divisions of study:
+ Division of Academic Affairs (University Parallel Degree Program)
+ Career & Technical programs
+ Health Sciences
+ Workforce Development

Hinds Community College at Utica (Utica, MS)

Founded in 1903, this public college offers four programs of study:
+ ABE/High School Equivalency
+ Academic programs (for credit transfers to a four-year university)*
+ Career and Technical programs
+ Nursing and Health-Related programs

Jackson State University (Jackson, MS)

Founded in 1877, this public university has six colleges of study and a graduate school:
+ College of Business
+ College of Education and Human Development
+ College of Liberal Arts
+ College of Public Service

+ College of Science, Engineering and Technology
+ School of Public Health

Mississippi Valley State University (Itta Bena, MS)

Founded in 1950, this public university has nine departments of study and a graduate school:
+ Business Administration
+ Criminal Justice
+ English and Foreign Languages
+ Fine Arts — Music & Design
+ Health, Physical Education, and Recreation
+ Mass Communication
+ Mathematics, Computer and Information Sciences
+ Natural Sciences and Environmental Health*
+ Social Sciences

Rust College (Holly Springs, MS)

Founded in 1866, this private college is religiously affiliated with the United Methodist Church.

Tougaloo College (Hinds College, MS)

Founded in 1869, this private college, religiously affiliated with the American Missionary Association, has four academic divisions of study:
+ Division of Education
+ Division of Humanities
+ Division of Natural Sciences
+ Division of Social Science

Missouri

Harris Stowe State University (St. Louis, MO)

Founded in 1857, this public university offers five programs of study:
+ Science, Technology, Engineering, and Math*
+ Health Care
+ Public Service

+ Business
+ Education

Lincoln University of Missouri (Jefferson City, MO)

Founded in 1866, this public university has five colleges of study and a graduate school:

+ College of Agriculture, Environmental and Human Sciences*
+ College of Arts and Sciences
+ School of Business
+ School of Education
+ School of Nursing

North Carolina

Bennett College (Greensboro, NC)

Founded in 1873, this private college, religiously affiliated with United Methodist Church, has nine departments of study:

+ Department of Biological and Chemical Sciences
+ Department of Humanities
+ Department of Mathematics and Computer Science
+ Department of Political Science and Sociology
+ Department of Psychology
+ Department of Business, Economics and Entrepreneurship
+ Department of Curriculum and Instruction
+ Department of Journalism and Media Studies
+ Department of Social Work

Elizabeth City State College (Elizabeth City, NC)

Founded in 1891, this public college has nine departments of study and a graduate school:

+ Department of Business and Economics
+ Department of Education, Psychology, and Health
+ Department of Language, Literature, and Communication
+ Department of Mathematics and Computer Science
+ Department of Military Science

+ Dr. Herman G. Cooke Department of Natural Sciences, Pharmacy, and Health Professions
+ Department of Social and Behavioral Sciences
+ Department of Technology
+ Department of Visual and Performing Arts

Fayetteville State University (Fayetteville, NC)

Founded in 1867, this public university has three colleges of study:

+ College of Arts and Sciences
+ Broadwell College of Business and Economics
+ College of Education

Johnson C. Smith University (Charlotte, NC)

Founded in 1867, this private university, religiously affiliated with the Presbyterian Church (USA), has three colleges of study:

+ College of Arts and Letters
+ College of STEM
+ College of Professional Studies

Livingstone College (Salisbury, NC)

Founded in 1879, this private college, religiously affiliated with AME Zion, offers four divisions of study:

+ Division of Business
+ Division of Education, Psychology & Social Work
+ Division of Liberal Arts & Humanities
+ Division of Mathematics & Science

North Carolina Agriculture & Technical State University (Greensboro, NC)

Founded in 1891, this public university has eight colleges of study and a graduate school:

+ College of Agriculture and Environmental Sciences*
+ College of Arts, Humanities and Social Sciences
+ College of Business and Economics

+ College of Education
+ College of Engineering
+ College of Health and Human Sciences
+ College of Science and Technology
+ The Joint School of Nanoscience and Nanoengineering

North Carolina Central University (Durham, NC)

Founded in 1910, this public university offers four colleges of study and has a graduate school and law school:
+ College of Arts & Sciences*
+ College of Behavioral & Social Sciences
+ School of Business
+ School of Education

Shaw University (Raleigh, NC)

Founded in 1865, this private university, religiously affiliated with National Baptist Convention, (US), offers eight academic divisions of study:
+ Business and Professional Studies
+ Communication and Humanities
+ Divinity School
+ Education and Social Work
+ General Education
+ Health and Human Sciences
+ Science and Technology
+ Social Sciences

St. Augustine's College (Raleigh, NC)

Founded in 1867, this private college, religiously affiliated with the Episcopal Church, has five schools of study:
+ School of Business, Management & Technology
+ School of Humanities, Education, Social & Behavioral Sciences
+ School of Sciences, Mathematics & Public Health

+ School of General Studies
+ Division of Military Science

Winston-Salem State University (Winston-Salem, NC)

Founded in 1892, this public university has two schools of study and a graduate school:
+ College of Arts, Sciences, Business and Education
+ School of Health Sciences

Ohio

Central State University (Wilberforce, OH)

Founded in 1887, this public university, religiously affiliated with the AME Church, has four colleges of study:
+ College of Business
+ College of Education
+ College of Humanities, Arts & Social Sciences
+ College of Engineering, Science, Technology & Agriculture*

Wilberforce University (Wilberforce, OH)

Founded in 1856, this private university, religiously affiliated with the AME Church, offers 23 majors and graduate, adult, and continuing education programs.

Oklahoma

Langston University (Langston, OK)

Founded in 1897, this public university has six schools and a graduate school:
+ Agriculture & Applied Sciences*
+ Arts & Sciences
+ Business
+ Education & Behavioral Sciences
+ Nursing & Health Professions
+ Physical Therapy

Pennsylvania

Cheyney University of Pennsylvania (Cheyney, PA)

Founded in 1837, this public university has two schools:
+ School of Arts & Sciences*
+ School of Education & Professional Studies

Lincoln University (Chester County, PA)

Founded in 1854, this public university offers 32 degrees and has a graduate school.

South Carolina

Allen University (Columbia, SC)

Founded in 1870, this private university, religiously affiliated with the AME Church, has seven divisions of study:
+ Biology
+ Business
+ English
+ Music
+ Mathematics
+ Religion
+ Social Studies

Benedict College (Columbia, SC)

Founded in 1870, this private college, religiously affiliated with American Baptist Church (USA), has five schools of study:
+ Tyrone Adam Burroughs School of Business and Entrepreneurship
+ School of Education, Health and Human Services
+ School of Humanities, Arts, and Social Sciences
+ School of Science, Technology, and Engineering*
+ School of Continuing Education

Claflin University (Orangeburg, SC)

Founded in 1869, this private university, religiously affiliated with United Methodist Church, has four schools of study:

+ School of Business
+ School of Education
+ School of Humanities and Social Sciences
+ School of Natural Sciences and Mathematics

Clinton Junior College (Rock Hill, SC)

Founded in 1894, this private college, religiously affiliated with AME Zion, offers eight degrees:

+ BS in Business Administration or Biology
+ BA in Religious Studies
+ Associate of Arts in Liberal Arts, Religious Studies, and Early Childhood Development
+ Associate of Science in Business Administration and Natural Sciences

Denmark Technical College (Denmark, SC)

Founded in 1947, this public college offers associate degrees and one-year diploma programs as well as technical certificates.

Morris College (Sumter, SC)

Founded in 1908, this private college, religiously affiliated with the Baptist Educational and Missionary Convention, has six academic divisions of study:

+ Division of General Studies
+ Division of Business Administration
+ Division of Education
+ Division of Religion and Humanities
+ Division of Natural Sciences and Mathematics
+ Division of Social Sciences

South Carolina State University (Orangeburg, SC)

Founded in 1896, this public university has 13 academic departments and a graduate program:

+ Department of Accounting, Agribusiness, & Economics
+ Department of Biological & Physical Sciences
+ Department of Business Administration
+ Department of Civil and Mechanical Engineering Technology & Nuclear Engineering
+ Department of Education
+ Department of English & Modern Languages
+ Department of Health Sciences
+ Department of Human Services
+ Department of Industrial & Electrical Engineering Technology
+ Department of Mathematics & Computer Science
+ Department of Military Science
+ Department of Social Science
+ Department of Visual & Performing Arts

Voorhees College (Denmark, SC)

Founded in 1897, this private college, religiously affiliated with the Episcopal Church, has three departments of study:

+ Department of Business and Entrepreneurship
+ Department of Science, Technology, Health & Human Services
+ Department of Humanities, Education, and Social Sciences

Tennessee

American Baptist College (Nashville, TN)

Founded in 1924, this private college, religiously affiliated with the Baptist Church, offers six degrees:

+ Associate of Arts in General Studies
+ BA in Bible & Theology
+ BA in Behavioral Studies
+ Bachelor of Theology

* BA in Entrepreneurial Leadership
* Associate of Arts in Music and Arts

Fisk University (Nashville, TN)

Founded in 1866, this private university, religiously affiliated with United Church of Christ, has two schools of study:
* School of Humanities and Behavioral Social Sciences
* School of Natural Sciences, Mathematics, and Business

Lane College (Jackson, TN)

Founded in 1882, this private college, religiously affiliated with Christian Methodist Episcopal Church, offers three divisions of study:
* Business and Social and Behavioral Science
* Liberal Studies and Education
* Natural and Physical Sciences

LeMoyne-Owen College (Memphis, TN)

Founded in 1862, this private college, religiously affiliated with United Church of Christ, has six divisions of study:
* Business & Economic Development
* Education
* Fine Arts & Humanities
* Natural & Mathematical Sciences
* Social & Behavioral Sciences
* Accelerated Studies

Meharry Medical College (Nashville, TN)

Founded in 1876, this private college, religiously affiliated with United Methodist Church, has two schools of study and graduate programs:
* School of Medicine
* School of Dentistry

Tennessee State University (Nashville, TN)

Founded in 1912, this public university has eight colleges and schools of study and a graduate school:
+ Agriculture*
+ Business
+ Education .
+ Engineering
+ Health Sciences
+ Liberal Arts
+ Life and Physical Sciences
+ Public Service

Texas

Huston-Tillotson University (Austin, TX)

Founded in 1875, this private university, religiously affiliated with the United Methodist Church/United Church of Christ, has nine departments of study:
+ Department of Educator Preparation
+ Department of English
+ Department of Kinesiology
+ Department of Humanities and Fine Arts
+ Department of Mathematics
+ Department of Natural Sciences*
+ Department of Social and Behavioral Sciences
+ Department of Business Administration
+ Department of Computer Science

Jarvis Christian College (Hawkins, TX)

Founded in 1912, this private college, religiously affiliated with the Disciples of Christ, offers:
+ Environmental Studies (as a minor)
+ Associate of Arts (3 degrees)
+ BA (4 degrees)
+ Bachelors of Business Administration (5 degrees)

+ BS (8 degrees)
+ BS Teacher Certification (10 degrees)

Paul Quinn College (Dallas, TX)

Founded in 1872, this private college, religiously affiliated with the AME Church, has six divisions of study:

+ Business Administration
+ Health and Wellness
+ Legal Studies
+ Liberal Arts
+ Liberal Arts — Path to Teacher Certification
+ Religious Studies

Prairie View A&M University (Prairie View, TX)

Founded in 1876, this public university has eight colleges and schools of study:

+ College of Agriculture and Human Services
+ Brailsford College of Arts and Sciences
+ College of Business
+ Whitlowe R. Green College of Education
+ Roy G. Perry College of Engineering
+ College of Juvenile Justice and Psychology
+ College of Nursing
+ School of Architecture

Southwestern Christian College (Terrell, TX)

Founded in 1948, this private college, religiously affiliated with the Church of Christ, offers an Associate of Arts, Associate of Science, or Bachelor of Science in Religious Studies.

St. Philip's College (San Antonio, TX)

Founded in 1898, this public college, religiously affiliated with the Episcopal Church, has 14 fields of study:

+ Allied Construction Trades
+ Business Information Solutions

- Communications and Learning/Liberal Arts
- Early Childhood and Family Studies
- Fine Arts/Kinesiology
- Health Sciences
- LVN and ADN Mobility
- Mathematics
- Natural Sciences*
- Social and Behavioral Sciences
- Tourism, Hospitality, and Culinary Arts
- Transportation and Manufacturing Technologies
- Transportation Services Technologies
- Vocational Nursing

Texas College (Tyler, TX)

Founded in 1894, this private college, religiously affiliated with Christian Methodist Episcopal Church, has four academic divisions:

- Business & Social Sciences
- General Studies & Humanities
- Interdisciplinary Studies (Teacher Education)
- Natural & Computational Sciences

Texas Southern University (Houston, TX)

Founded in 1927, this public university has seven colleges of study, a graduate school, and a law school:

- Jesse H. Jones School of Business
- Barbara Jordan-Mickey Leland School of Public Affairs
- College of Education
- College of Science, Engineering, and Technology
- College of Liberal Arts & Behavioral Sciences
- College of Pharmacy & Health Services
- School of Communication

Wiley College (Marshall, TX)

Founded in 1873, this private college, religiously affiliated with the United Methodist Church, has 4 schools of study:
+ Social Sciences & Humanities
+ Business & Technology
+ Education
+ Sciences

US Virgin Islands

University of the Virgin Islands (St. Croix & St. Thomas, VI)

Founded in 1962, this public university has five colleges and schools of study:
+ School of Business
+ School of Education
+ School of Nursing
+ College of Liberal Arts & Social Sciences
+ College of Science & Mathematics*

Virginia

Hampton University (Hampton, VA)

Founded in 1868, this private university has seven colleges of study and a graduate school:
+ Business
+ Engineering & Technology
+ Journalism & Communications
+ Liberal Arts & Education
+ Nursing
+ Pharmacy
+ Science*

Norfolk State University (Norfolk, VA)

Founded in 1935, this public university has five schools of study and a graduate program:
+ College of Liberal Arts
+ College of Science, Engineering, and Technology
+ Ethelyn R. Strong School of Social Work
+ School of Business
+ School of Education

Virginia State University (Petersburg, VA)

Founded in 1882, this public university has six colleges of study:
+ College of Engineering and Technology
+ College of Natural and Health Sciences
+ College of Agriculture*
+ College of Education
+ College of Humanities and Social Sciences
+ Reginald F. Lewis College of Business

Virginia Union University (Richmond, VA)

Founded in 1865, this private university, religiously affiliated with the American Baptist Church, has three schools of study:
+ Sydney Lewis School of Business
+ Evelyn R. Syphax School of Education, Psychology, and Interdisciplinary Studies
+ School of Arts & Sciences

Virginia University of Lynchburg (Lynchburg, VA)

Founded in 1886, this private university, religiously affiliated with the Baptist Church, has three schools of study:
+ G.W. Hayes School of Arts and Sciences
+ School of Business
+ School of Religion

West Virginia

Bluefield State College (Bluefield, WV)

Founded in 1895, this public college (13% black, 80% white) has five schools of study:

- Arts & Sciences
- Business
- Education
- Engineering, Technology, & Computer Science
- Nursing & Allied Health

West Virginia State University (Institute, WV)

Founded in 1891, this public university has four colleges of study:

- College of Arts & Humanities
- College of Business and Social Sciences
- College of Natural Sciences and Mathematics
- College of Professional Studies

Appendix 3

Hispanic-Serving Institutions (HSIs)

To be an HSI, a university must have at least 25% Hispanic undergrad full-time students. Full federal definition available here: https://www2.ed.gov/print/programs/idueshsi/definition.html

Note: Percentage Hispanic numbers originate from the Hispanic Association of Colleges & Universities 2017–18 database. (https://www.hacu.net/hacu/HSIs.asp)

Several of these colleges have multiple campuses (especially CA), so for this list they were treated individually as they seemed to have different academic program offerings.

Environmental degrees strictly focus on an environmental aspect. As such, degrees like agriculture, aquaculture, marine biology, and environmental science count, whereas chemistry and (ordinary) biology do not.

An asterisk (*) indicates that one or several environmental degrees are available under the school/program of study.

Each state name also has a number next to it representing how many HSI's are currently in the state.

Arizona (16)

Arizona State University, West (Phoenix, AZ)

This four-year public university, 33% Hispanic, has seven colleges of study and a graduate school:

- W.P. Carey School of Business
- Thunderbird School of Global Management

- College of Health Solutions
- New College of Interdisciplinary Arts & Sciences*
- College of Nursing and Health Innovation
- College of Public Service and Community Solutions
- Mary Lou Fulton Teachers College

Arizona Western College (Yuma, AZ)

This two-year public college, 73% Hispanic, offers eight programs of study:

- General Education
- Arts, Humanities, & Communication
- Business & Computers
- Education
- Healthcare & Public Safety
- Science, Agriculture, Engineering, & Math*
- Social & Behavioral Sciences
- Technology, Trades, & Food Science

Estrella Mountain Community College (Avondale, AZ)

This two-year public college, 53% Hispanic, has 11 departments of study:

- Arts, Communications, & Languages
- Business, Finance, Management, & Marketing
- Education
- Food, Hospitality, and Tourism
- Healthcare & Wellness
- History & Humanities
- Human & Social Services
- Information Technology
- Administration of Justice Studies
- Manufacturing, Distribution, & Energy*
- STEM

University of Arizona, South (Tucson, AZ)

This four-year public university, 42% Hispanic, has 12 programs of study:
+ Applied Sciences
+ Arts & Media
+ Business
+ Cybersecurity
+ Data & Record Studies
+ Education
+ Health & Wellness
+ Language & Cultures
+ Law & Public Policy
+ Public Service
+ Social & Behavioral Sciences
+ Technology & Information

Arkansas (1)

Cossatot Community College of the University of Arkansas (De Queen, AR)

This two-year public college, 27% Hispanic, has 11 programs of study:
+ Agriculture
+ Business
+ Communications
+ Criminal Justice
+ Dental Hygiene
+ Radiology/Imaging Science
+ Education
+ Medical
+ Psychology
+ STEM
+ Skilled & Technical Programs

California (170)

Azusa Pacific University (Azusa, CA)

This four-year private university, 32% Hispanic, has nine schools of study:

- Accounting
- Arts
- Behavioral and Applied Sciences
- Business and Management
- Education
- Liberal Arts and Sciences
- Nursing
- Seminary
- Theology

California Lutheran University (Thousand Oaks, CA)

This four-year private university, 32% Hispanic, has five colleges of study and two graduate schools:

- College of Arts & Sciences*
- School of Management
- Pacific Lutheran Theological Seminary
- Graduate School of Education
- Graduate School of Psychology

California State Polytechnic University (Pomona, CA)

This four-year public university, 43% Hispanic, has eight colleges of study:

- Don B. Huntley College of Agriculture*
- College of Business Administration
- College of Education & Integrative Studies
- College of Engineering
- College of Environmental Design
- Collins College of Hospitality Management
- College of Letters, Arts, and Social Sciences
- College of Science

California State University, Bakersfield (Bakersfield, CA)

This four-year public university, 57% Hispanic, has four schools of study:
+ Arts & Humanities
+ Business and Public Administration
+ Natural Sciences, Mathematics, and Engineering
+ Social Sciences and Education

California State University, Channel Islands (Camarillo, CA)

This four-year public university, 50% Hispanic, has 27 programs of study, including Environmental Science & Resource Management* (1 degree with concentrations in either ES or RM).

California State University, Chico (Chico, CA)

This four-year public university, 33% Hispanic, has seven colleges of study and a graduate school:
+ College of Agriculture
+ College of Behavioral & Social Sciences
+ College of Business
+ College of Communication & Education
+ College of Engineering, Computer Science, & Construction Management
+ College of Humanities & Fine Arts
+ College of Natural Sciences*

California State University, Dominguez Hills (Carson, CA)

This four-year public university, 63% Hispanic, has five colleges of study:
+ College of Arts & Humanities
+ College of Business Administration & Public Policy
+ College of Education
+ College of Natural & Behavioral Sciences*
+ College of Health, Human Services, & Nursing

California State University, Fresno (Fresno, CA)

This four-year public university, 52% Hispanic, has eight colleges of study:

- College of Arts & Humanities
- College of Health and Human Services
- College of Science and Mathematics*
- College of Social Sciences
- Craig School of Business
- Jordan College of Agricultural Sciences and Technology*
- Kremen School of Education and Human Development
- Lyles College of Engineering

California State University, Fullerton (Fullerton, CA)

This four-year public university, 43% Hispanic, has eight colleges of study:

- Arts
- Business and Economics
- Communications
- Education
- Engineering and Computer Science
- Health and Human Development
- Humanities and Social Sciences*
- Natural Sciences and Mathematics

California State University, Long Beach (Long Beach, CA)

This four-year public university, 42% Hispanic, has seven colleges of study:

- College of the Arts
- College of Business
- College of Education
- College of Engineering
- College of Health & Human Services
- College of Liberal Arts*
- College of Natural Sciences & Mathematics

California State University, Los Angeles (Los Angeles, CA)

This four-year public university, 66% Hispanic, has six colleges of study:
+ College of Arts and Letters
+ College of Business and Economics
+ Charter College of Education
+ College of Engineering, Computer Science, and Technology
+ Rongxiang Xu College of Health and Human Services
+ College of Natural and Social Services*

California State University, Monterey Bay (Seaside, CA)

This four-year public university, 47% Hispanic, has five colleges of study:
+ College of Arts, Humanities, and Social Sciences
+ College of Business
+ College of Education
+ College of Health Sciences and Human Services
+ College of Science*

California State University, Northridge (Northridge, CA)

This four-year public university, 49% Hispanic, has nine colleges of study:
+ Mike Curb College of Arts, Media, & Communication
+ David Nazarian College of Business and Economics
+ Michael D. Eisner College of Education
+ Engineering & Computer Science
+ Health & Human Development
+ Humanities
+ Science & Mathematics
+ Social & Behavioral Sciences
+ Tseng College

California State University, San Bernardino (San Bernardino, CA)

This four-year public university, 64% Hispanic, has five colleges of study:
+ College of Arts & Letters
+ College of Business & Public Administration

- College of Education
- College of Natural Sciences
- College of Social & Behavioral Sciences*

California State University, San Marcos (San Marcos, CA)

This four-year public university, 44% Hispanic, has four colleges of study and a graduate school:
- College of Humanities, Arts, Behavioral & Social Sciences*
- College of Business Administration
- College of Education, Health & Human Services
- College of Science & Mathematics

California State University Stanislaus (Turlock, CA)

This four-year public university, 53% Hispanic, has four colleges of study:
- College of the Arts, Humanities, & Social Sciences*
- College of Education, Kinesiology, and Social Work
- College of Science
- College of Business Administration

Fresno Pacific University (Fresno, CA)

This four-year private university, 48% Hispanic, offers 34 degrees, including Environmental Science and Studies* (separate degrees).

Mills College (Oakland, CA)

This four-year private university, 28% Hispanic, offers 33 undergrad degrees, including Environmental Science and Studies,* and has a graduate school.

Mount Saint Mary's University (Los Angeles, CA)

This four-year private university, 64% Hispanic, offers 32 majors of study, associate degrees and a graduate program.

Porterville College (Porterville, CA)

This two-year public college, 77% Hispanic, offers the following:
+ Associate in Science (8 degrees)
+ Associate in Arts (6 degrees)
+ Associate in Science for transfer degrees (AS-T) (5 degrees)
+ Associate in Arts for transfer degrees (AA-T) (8 degrees)
+ Certificates of Completion and Achievement
+ Job Skill Certificates

Saint Mary's College of California (Moraga, CA)

This four-year private college, 28% Hispanic, has four schools of study:
+ School of Liberal Arts
+ School of Science*
+ School of Economics and Business Administration
+ Kalmanovitz School of Education

San Diego State University (San Diego, CA)

This four-year public university, 30% Hispanic, has seven colleges of study and a graduate school:
+ College of Arts and Letters
+ College of Engineering
+ College of Professional Studies and Fine Arts
+ Fowler College of Business
+ College of Education
+ College of Health and Human Services
+ College of Sciences*

University of California, Irvine (Irvine, CA)

This four-year public university, 27% Hispanic, has 12 divisions of study and a law school:
+ Arts
+ Biological Sciences
+ Business
+ Education

- Engineering
- Humanities
- Information & Computer Sciences
- Interdisciplinary Studies*
- Physical Sciences*
- Social Ecology
- Social Sciences
- Susan and Henry Samueli College of Health Sciences

University of California, Merced (Merced, CA)

This four-year public university, 53% Hispanic, offers 24 degrees, including Environmental Engineering (BS)* and 25 minors, as well as 17 graduate programs.

University of California, Riverside (Riverside, CA)

This four-year public university, 41% Hispanic, has six colleges of study and a graduate school of education:
- Marlan and Rosemary Bourns College of Engineering*
- College of Humanities, Arts, and Social Sciences
- College of Natural and Agricultural Sciences*
- School of Business
- School of Medicine
- School of Public Policy

University of California, Santa Barbara (Santa Barbara, CA)

This four-year public university, 27% Hispanic, has five colleges of study and a graduate school:
- College of Letters & Science
- College of Engineering
- College of Creative Studies
- Bren School of Environmental Science and Management*
- Gevirtz Graduate School of Education

University of California, Santa Cruz (Santa Cruz, CA)

This four-year public university, 28% Hispanic, has five divisions of study:

- Art
- Humanities
- Physical and Biological Sciences*
- Social Sciences*
- Jack Baskin School of Engineering

University of La Verne (La Verne, CA)

This four-year private university, 53% Hispanic, has three colleges of study, as well as a college of law:

- College of Arts and Sciences
- College of Business and Public Management
- LaFetra College of Education

Whittier College (Whittier, CA)

This four-year private university, 50% Hispanic, has 32 majors, including Environmental Science & Environmental Studies* (2 majors) and 39 minors.

Colorado (13)

Adams State University (Alamosa, CO)

This four-year public university, 38% Hispanic, offers programs in 12 areas:

- Administration
- Business
- Counseling
- Education
- Health
- Human Performance
- Humanities
- Language & Communications
- Liberal Arts

- Science & Math
- Social & Behavioral Science
- Visual & Performance Arts

Colorado State University–Pueblo (Pueblo, CO)

This four-year public university, 33% Hispanic, has five schools of study and a graduate school:
- College of Education, Engineering, and Professional Studies
- College of Humanities and Social Sciences
- College of Science and Mathematics*
- Hasan School of Business
- School of Nursing

Pueblo Community College (Pueblo, CO)

This four-year public college, 32% Hispanic, offers a wide variety of programs for associate degrees and certificates. Also offers limited Bachelor of Applied Science in:
- Computed Tomography
- Dental Hygiene
- Magnetic Resonance Imaging

Trinidad State Junior College (Trinidad, CO)

This two-year public college, 46% Hispanic, offers over 50 degrees in various academic and professional areas at two campuses in Trinidad and Alamosa, CO.

Connecticut (6)

Capital Community College (Hartford, CT)

This two-year public college, 30% Hispanic, has six departments of study:
- Business & Technology
- Health Careers & Public Safety
- Humanities
- Nursing

+ Science & Mathematics
+ Social & Behavioral Sciences

Naugatuck Valley Community College (Waterbury, CT)

This two-year public college, 31% Hispanic, has four divisions of study:
+ Allied Health, Nursing, and Physical Education
+ Liberal Arts/Behavioral and Social Sciences
+ Business
+ STEM* (Environmental degree is AS)

Norwalk Community College (Norwalk, CT)

This two-year public college, 38% Hispanic, offers 10 departments of study:
+ Art, Architecture + Design
+ Business
+ Computer Science
+ English
+ English as a Second Language
+ Humanities
+ Mathematics + Engineering
+ Nursing and Allied Health
+ Science
+ Social and Behavioral Science

University of Connecticut, Stamford (Stamford, CT)

This four-year public university, 27% Hispanic, offers 11 programs of study:
+ Business
+ Certificate Entry into Nursing
+ Computer Science
+ Digital Media and Design
+ Economics
+ English
+ General Studies
+ History

+ Human Development and Family Studies
+ Political Studies
+ Psychology

District of Columbia, Washington (1)

Trinity Washington University (Washington, DC)

This four-year private university, 28% Hispanic, has five colleges of study and a graduate school:

+ College of Arts & Sciences
+ School of Business & Graduate Studies
+ School of Education
+ School of Professional Studies
+ School of Nursing & Health Professions

Florida (25)

Florida International University (Miami, FL)

This four-year public university, 66% Hispanic, has nine colleges of study, a graduate school, and law school:

+ Arts, Sciences, and Education*
+ Business
+ Chaplin School of Hospitality and Tourism Management
+ Communication, Architecture + The Arts
+ Engineering & Computing
+ Herbert Wertheim College of Medicine
+ Nicole Wertheim College of Nursing & Health Sciences
+ Robert Stempel College of Public Health & Social Work
+ Steven J. Green School of International and Public Affairs

Miami Dade College (Miami, FL)

This four-year public college, 70% Hispanic, has 11 schools of study, the Law Center, Idea Center, Animation & Gaming International Complex, Culinary and Fashion Institutes, and International Hospitality Center:

+ School of Architecture and Interior Design
+ School of Aviation

- School of Business
- School of Education
- School of Engineering and Technology
- School of Entertainment and Design Technology
- Funeral Service Education
- School of Health Services
- School of Justice
- School of Nursing
- School of Science* (associate degree in environmental studies)

Polytechnic College of Puerto Rico, Miami (Miami, FL)

This four-year private college, 93% Hispanic, offers the following degrees:
- Bachelor of Business Administration
- Bachelor of Science in Organizational Management
- Bachelor of Science in Computer Science
- Bachelor of Arts in Computer Science
- Master of Business Administration
- Master of Engineering Management

Polytechnic College of Puerto Rico, Orlando (Orlando, FL)

This four-year private college, 97% Hispanic, offers the following degrees:
- Bachelor of Business Administration
- BS in Organizational Management
- BS in Civil Engineering
- BS in Computer Engineering
- BS in Computer Science
- BS in Electrical Engineering with concentration in Communication Signal and Control
- BS in Electrical Engineering with concentration in Power
- BS in Environmental Engineering*
- BS in Mechanical Engineering
- Master of Business Administration
- Master of Engineering Management

Georgia (2)

Altierus Career College–Norcross (Norcross, GA)

This two-year private college, 25% Hispanic, offers the following programs:

+ Computer Information Technology
+ Dental Assistant
+ Electrical Technician
+ Heating, Ventilation, and Air Conditioning
+ Massage Therapy
+ Medical Assistant
+ Medical Billing and Coding
+ Nursing Associate of Science
+ Pharmacy Technician
+ Surgical Technologist

Dalton State College (Dalton, GA)

This four-year public college, 25% Hispanic, has five colleges of study:

+ Wright School of Business
+ School of Education
+ School of Health Professions
+ School of Liberal Arts
+ School of Science, Technology, and Mathematics

Illinois (25)

College of Lake County (Grayslake, IL)

This two-year public college, 38% Hispanic, has six divisions of study:

+ Adult Education and ESL
+ Biological and Health Sciences
+ Business and Social Sciences
+ Communication, Arts, Humanities, and Fine Arts
+ Engineering, Math and Physical Sciences*
+ Workforce and Personal Development Institute

Dominican University (River Forest, IL)

This four-year private university, 52% Hispanic, has seven colleges of study:

- ✦ Rosary College of Arts and Sciences*
- ✦ Brennan School of Business
- ✦ Borra College of Health Sciences
- ✦ College of Applied Social Sciences
- ✦ School of Education
- ✦ School of Information Studies
- ✦ School of Social Work

Morton College (Cicero, IL)

This two-year public college,85% Hispanic, has eight departments of study:

- ✦ Communications
- ✦ Business Technologies
- ✦ Health Occupations
- ✦ Humanities and Fine Arts
- ✦ Mathematics
- ✦ Sciences
- ✦ Social and Behavioral Sciences
- ✦ Technical Occupations

Saint Augustine College (Chicago, IL)

This four-year private college, 89% Hispanic, has five departments of study:

- ✦ Department of Social Work and Addictions Studies
- ✦ Department of Business, CIS, and Culinary Arts
- ✦ Department of Languages, Literature, and Humanities
- ✦ Department of Early Childhood Education and Social Sciences
- ✦ Department of Sciences and Health

Saint Xavier University (Chicago, IL)

This four-year private university, 39% Hispanic, has three schools of study:

+ College of Arts and Sciences
+ Graham School of Management
+ School of Nursing and Health Sciences

Waubonsee Community College (Chicago, IL)

This two-year public college, 34% Hispanic, offers 10 programs of study:

+ Arts, Design, and Humanities
+ Business
+ Communications and World Languages
+ Education
+ Health Sciences
+ Industry and Manufacturing
+ Public Safety and Service
+ STEM
+ Social and Behavioral Sciences
+ Developmental Education

Indiana (2)

Calumet College of Saint Joseph (Whiting, IN)

This four-year private college, 31% Hispanic, has seven departments of study:

+ Behavioral & Social Sciences
+ Biophysical Chemistry & Math
+ Business Management
+ Education
+ Humanities
+ Public Safety & Criminal Justice
+ General Education

Horizon University (Indianapolis, IN)

This four-year private university, 26% Hispanic, offers the following degrees:

+ Bachelor in Biblical Studies
+ Bachelor in Leadership and Ministry
+ Bachelor in Organizational Leadership
+ Associate in Biblical Studies
+ Certificate in Chaplaincy
+ Certificate in Biblical Counseling
+ Certificate in TESOL (Teaching English to Speakers of Other Languages)

Kansas (4)

[Note: Three colleges are on accreditation probation or notice]

Seward County Community College (Liberal, KS)

This two-year public college, 51% Hispanic, has five divisions of study:

+ Allied Health
+ Industrial Technology
+ Agriculture, Business, & Personal Services*
+ Humanities and Social Sciences
+ Science, Math, and PE

Louisiana (1)

Saint Joseph Seminary College (Saint Benedict, LA)

This four-year private college, 32% Hispanic, offers two BA's and a pre-theology program:

+ Philosophy + Liberal Arts
+ Philosophy + Theology

Massachusetts (5)

Northern Essex Community College (Essex County, MA)

This two-year public college, 42% Hispanic, offers 14 programs of study:

+ Art and Design
+ Business

- Communication Arts
- Computer & Information Sciences
- Criminal Justice
- Deaf Studies
- Education
- General Studies
- Health
- Human Services
- Liberal Arts
- Performing Arts
- Science*
- Technology & Engineering

Urban College of Boston (Boston, MA)

This two-year private college, 65% Hispanic, offers associate degrees and certificates:

- Early Childhood Education
- Human Services Administration
- General Studies
- Health and Nutrition (Certificate only)

Minnesota (1)

University of St Thomas (St. Paul, MN)

This four-year private university, 45% Hispanic, has seven colleges of study and a Graduate School of Professional Psychology:

- College of Arts & Sciences*
- Opus College of Business
- School of Education
- Dougherty Family College
- St. Paul Seminary School of Divinity
- School of Engineering
- School of Law
- School of Social Work

Nevada (4)

College of Southern Nevada (Clark County, NV)

This four-year public college, 32% Hispanic, offers eight divisions of study:

- Advanced & Applied Technologies
- Arts & Letters
- Business, Hospitality, & Public Services
- Education, Behavioral & Social Sciences
- Health Sciences
- Science & Mathematics
- Division of Workforce & Economic Development
- Apprenticeship Studies

Truckee Meadows Community College (Reno, NV)

This two-year public college, 29% Hispanic, offers four divisions of study:

- Business and Social Sciences Division
- Liberal Arts Division
- Sciences Division
- Technical Sciences Division

New Jersey (17)

Hudson County Community College (Hudson County, NJ)

This two-year public college, 56% Hispanic, offers five divisions of study:

- Business, Culinary Arts, and Hospitality Management
- Humanities
- Nursing and Health Sciences
- STEM*
- Social Sciences

Middlesex County College (Edison, NJ)

This two-year public college, 32% Hispanic, has two divisions of study:

- Division of Arts and Sciences
- Division of Professional Studies*

Montclair State University (Montclair, NJ)

This four-year public university, 28% Hispanic, offers nine colleges of study and a graduate school:

+ College of the Arts
+ College of Education and Human Services
+ College of Humanities and Social Sciences
+ College of Science and Mathematics
+ Feliciano School of Business
+ John J. Cali School of Music
+ New Jersey School of Conservation*
+ School of Communication and Media
+ School of Nursing

New Jersey City University (Jersey City, NJ)

This four-year public university, 40% Hispanic, has four schools of study:

+ School of Business
+ College of Professional Studies
+ William J. Maxwell College of Arts & Sciences*
+ Deborah Cannon Partridge Wolfe College of Education

Rutgers, the State University of New Jersey (Newark, NJ)

This four-year public university, 28% Hispanic, has four schools of study, a graduate school, and law school:

+ Newark College of Arts and Sciences*
+ School of Criminal Justice
+ Rutgers Business School
+ School of Public Affairs & Administration

Saint Peter's University (Jersey City, NJ)

This four-year private university, 45% Hispanic, has four schools of study:

+ College of Arts & Sciences
+ School of Business Administration

+ School of Education
+ School of Nursing

New Mexico (23)

Central New Mexico Community College (Albuquerque, NM)

This two-year public college, 52% Hispanic, has six schools of study:
+ Adult & General Education
+ Applied Technologies
+ Business & Information Technology
+ Communication, Humanities, & Social Sciences
+ Health, Wellness, & Public Safety
+ Math, Science, and Engineering

Clovis Community College (Clovis, NM)

This two-year public college, 40% Hispanic, offers 21 degree and certificate programs.

Luna Community College (Las Vegas, NM)

This two-year public college, 79% Hispanic, has seven programs of study:
+ Education
+ Nursing
+ Humanities
+ Allied Health
+ Vocational
+ STEM
+ Business

New Mexico Highlands University (Las Vegas, NM)

This four-year public university, 59% Hispanic, has four schools of study and a graduate school:
+ College of Arts & Sciences*
+ School of Business, Media, & Technology
+ School of Education
+ School of Social Work

New Mexico State University (Las Cruces, NM)

This four-year public university, 59% Hispanic, has six colleges of study and a graduate school:

+ College of Agricultural, Consumer, and Environmental Sciences*
+ College of Arts and Sciences
+ College of Business
+ College of Education
+ College of Engineering
+ College of Health and Social Services

Northern New Mexico College (Española, NM)

This two-year public college, 67% Hispanic, has five colleges of study:

+ College of Arts and Sciences*
+ College of Business Administration
+ College of Education
+ College of Engineering and Technology
+ College of Nursing and Health Sciences

University of New Mexico (Albuquerque, NM)

This four-year public university, 48% Hispanic, has 11 colleges of study and a graduate school:

+ Anderson School of Management
+ College of Arts & Sciences*
+ College of Education
+ College of Fine Arts
+ College of Nursing
+ College of Pharmacy
+ College of Population Health
+ School of Architecture and Planning
+ School of Engineering
+ School of Law
+ School of Medicine

Western New Mexico University (Silver City, NM)

This four-year public university, 48% Hispanic, offers a wide variety of associate, undergraduate, and graduate degrees, including Forest & Wildlife, Forest & Wildlife Law Enforcement, and Sustainable Development.*

New York (34)

American Musical and Dramatic Academy
(New York City, NY and Los Angeles, CA)

This four-year private academy, 26% Hispanic, offers the following programs:
+ Acting
+ Music Theater
+ Dance Theater
+ Performing Arts

Boricua College (New York, NY)

This four-year private college, 83% Hispanic, offers the following degrees:
+ Bachelor and Master of Science in Human Services
+ Bachelor of Science in Childhood Education
+ Master of Science in TESOL Education
+ Bilingual Education Extension Certificate (1–6, K–12)
+ Bachelor of Science in Business Administration
+ Bachelor of Arts in Liberal Arts and Sciences
+ Bachelor of Arts in Inter-American Studies
+ Master of Arts in Latin American and Caribbean Studies

College of Mount Saint Vincent (Bronx, NY)

This four-year private college, 42% Hispanic, offers a wide variety of academic programs.

John Jay College of Criminal Justice, CUNY (New York, NY)

This two-year public college, 51% Hispanic, offers approximately 50 majors, most with a focus on criminal justice.

Lehman College, CUNY (Bronx, NY)

This four-year public college, 58% Hispanic, has four schools of study:
+ School of Arts & Humanities
+ School of Education
+ School of Health Sciences, Human Services, and Nursing
+ School of Natural and Social Sciences*

Nyack College (New York, NY)

This four-year private college, 29% Hispanic, has eight colleges of study and a graduate school:
+ College of Arts & Sciences
+ College of Bible & Christian Ministry
+ School of Business & Leadership
+ School of Education
+ School of Music
+ School of Nursing
+ School of Social Work

Stella and Charles Guttman Community College (New York, NY)

This two-year public college, 60% Hispanic, offers the following programs:
+ Associate in Arts (5 degrees)
+ Associate in Applied Science for Information Technology

Vaughn College of Aeronautics and Technology (Queens, NY)

This four-year private college, 33% Hispanic, offers four areas of study:
+ Aviation Technology
+ Aviation
+ Management
+ Engineering & Technology

North Carolina (1)

Sampson Community College (Clinton, NC)

This two-year public college, 28% Hispanic, offers the following academic programs in addition to Workforce Development & Continuing Education, HS Equivalency Diploma, and English as a Second Language:

+ Arts & Science Programs
+ Education Programs·
+ Applied Technical Programs
+ Healthcare Programs
+ Business & Technology Programs
+ Public Service Programs

Ohio (1)

Union Institute & University (Cincinnati, OH)

This four-year private university, 26% Hispanic, offers seven degrees:

+ Bachelor of Business
+ Bachelor of Education
+ Bachelor of Social Science
+ Master of Arts
+ Master of Business
+ Master of Counseling
+ Doctor of Interdisciplinary Studies

Oklahoma (2)

Oklahoma Panhandle State University (Goodwell, OK)

This four-year public university, 26% Hispanic, has three colleges of study:

+ Agriculture, Science, and Nursing*
+ Business and Technology
+ Arts and Education

Randall University (Moore, OK)

This four-year private university, 26% Hispanic, has three schools of study and a graduate school:
  + School of Arts and Sciences
  + School of Christian Ministry
  + School of Education

Oregon (5)

Treasure Valley Community College (Ontario, OR)

This two-year public college, 25% Hispanic, offers 11 departments of study:
  + Agriculture & Natural Resources*
  + Aviation
  + Business & Computer Science
  + Career & Technical Education
  + Education
  + English & Humanities
  + Fine & Performing Arts
  + Health Professions
  + Math
  + Science
  + Social Science

Warner Pacific College (Portland, OR)

This four-year private college, 31% Hispanic, offers a wide variety of degrees and programs and has a graduate school.

Pennsylvania (1)

Reading Area Community College (Reading, PA)

This two-year public college, 34% Hispanic, offers five divisions of study:
  + Business
  + Communications, Arts and Humanities
  + Health Professions

+ Social Sciences/Human Services
+ STEM

Puerto Rico (63)

If you have an interest in PR, I encourage you to do your own research.

Texas (93)

Hallmark University (San Antonio, TX)

This four-year private university, 48% Hispanic, has four divisions of study:

+ Aeronautics
+ Business
+ Healthcare
+ Information Technology

Laredo Community College (Laredo, TX)

This two-year public college, 98% Hispanic, offers three divisions of study:

+ Arts & Sciences
+ Health Services
+ Workforce Education

St. Edwards University (Austin, TX)

This four-year private university, 41% Hispanic, has five schools of study:

+ School of Arts and Humanities
+ School of Human Development and Education
+ School of Behavioral and Social Sciences*
+ School of Natural Sciences *
+ Bill Munday School of Business

St. Mary's University (San Antonio, TX)

This four-year private university, 68% Hispanic, has three schools of study and a law school:

+ Greehey School of Business
+ School of Humanities and Social Sciences
+ School of Science, Engineering, and Technology*

South Texas College (McAllen, TX)

This four-year public college, 94% Hispanic, offers the following programs:

+ Bachelor of Applied Technology (Computer & Information Technologies; Technology Management; Medical and Health Services Management)
+ Bachelor of Applied Sciences (Organizational Leadership)
+ Associate Degree in Business & Technology
+ Associate Degree in Fine and Performing Arts
+ Associate Degree in Humanities
+ Associate Degree in Math & Science
+ Associate Degree in Nursing & Allied Health
+ Associate Degree in Social & Behavioral Sciences

Texas A&M International University (Laredo, TX)

This four-year public university, 95% Hispanic, has four colleges of study:

+ A.R. Sanchez School of Business
+ College of Arts and Sciences
+ College of Education
+ College of Nursing and Health Sciences

Texas A&M University–Kingsville (Kingsville, TX)

This four-year public university, 72% Hispanic, has five colleges of study and a graduate school:

+ College of Agriculture, Natural Resources, and Human Sciences*

- College of Arts and Sciences
- College of Business Administration
- Collee of Education and Human Performance
- College of Engineering

University of Texas at El Paso (El Paso, TX)

This four-year public university, 83% Hispanic, has eight colleges of study and a graduate school:
- College of Business Administration
- College of Education
- College of Engineering
- College of Health Sciences
- College of Liberal Arts*
- College of Science
- School of Nursing
- School of Pharmacy

University of Texas Rio Grande Valley (Harlingen, TX)

This four-year public university, 91% Hispanic, has 10 colleges of study and a graduate school:
- College of Education & P-16 Integration
- College of Engineering & Computer Science
- College of Fine Arts
- College of Health Professions
- College of Liberal Arts
- College of Sciences*
- Robert C. Vacker College of Business & Entrepreneurship
- School of Medicine
- School of Nursing
- School of Social Work

University of the Incarnate Word (San Antonio, TX)

This four-year private university, 58% Hispanic, has seven colleges of study:

+ College of Humanities, Arts, and Social Sciences
+ Dreeben School of Education
+ H-E-B School of Business and Administration
+ Ila Faye Miller School of Nursing and Health Professions
+ School of Math, Science, and Engineering
+ School of Media & Design
+ School of Professional Studies

Utah (1)

Stevens-Henager College (Ogden, Utah)

This four-year private college, 26% Hispanic, has four schools of study:

+ School of Healthcare
+ School of Business
+ School of Technology
+ School of Graphic Arts

Washington (5)

Heritage University (Toppenish, WA)

This four-year private university, 69% Hispanic, offers 21 undergrad degrees, including Environmental Studies*, and 5 graduate degrees.

Wenatchee Valley College (Wenatchee, WA)

This two-year public college, 39% Hispanic, offers six areas of study:

+ Health & Human Services
+ Liberal Arts
+ Business
+ STEM*
+ Skilled Trades
+ Exploratory

Yakima Valley College (Yakima, WA)

This four-year public college, 50% Hispanic, offers six degree pathways:
+ Arts & Humanities
+ Business
+ Exploratory
+ Healthcare
+ Social Sciences & Education
+ STEM

Wisconsin (1)

Alverno College (Milwaukee, WI)

This four-year private college, 28% Hispanic, has three divisions of study and a graduate school:
+ School of Arts & Sciences*
+ School of Professional Studies
+ School of Nursing

Appendix 4

Tribal Colleges and Universities

A LL LISTED COLLEGES were accredited at time of writing, but one should check again to make sure before applying.

An asterisk (*) indicates that one or several environmental degrees are available under the school/program of study.

Environmental degrees strictly focus on an environmental aspect. As such, degrees like agriculture, aquaculture, marine biology, and environmental science count, whereas chemistry and (ordinary) biology do not.

Alaska

Ilisagvik College (Utqiagvik, AK)

Founded in 1996, this college offers several areas of study:
+ Associate of Arts Degree (for transfer to a four-year university)
+ Teachers for the Arctic (early childhood, elementary, secondary)
+ Iñupiaq Studies
+ Allied Health
+ Business
+ Information Technology
+ Emergency Services
+ Vocational Trade
+ Heavy Equipment Operations
+ Community & Workforce Development
+ Foundation Studies (Reading, Writing, Math)

Arizona

Diné College (Tsaile, AZ)

Founded in 1968, this college has four schools of study:
+ School of Arts, Humanities, and English
+ School of Diné Studies and Education
+ School of Science, Technology, Engineering, and Math*
+ School of Business and Social Science

Tohono O'odham Community College (Sells, AZ)

Founded in 1998, this college offers transfer programs in the following areas:
+ Arts
+ Business
+ Science and Health*
+ Education
+ Liberal Arts
+ Social Services

It also offers direct employment programs in Building and Construction, Associate of Applied Sciences degrees, and certificates of training.

Kansas

Haskell Indian Nations University (Lawrence, KS)

Founded in 1884, this university has three colleges of study:
+ College of Humanities
+ College of Natural and Social Sciences*
+ Professional Schools (includes Business; Education; Health, Sport, and Exercise Science)

Michigan

Bay Mills Community College (Brimley, MI)

Founded in 1981, this college offers 30 courses that can lead to certificates and the following degrees:

+ Associate of Applied Science
+ Associate of Arts
+ Associate of Science
+ Bachelor of Arts

Keweenaw Bay Ojibwa Community College (Baraga, MI)

Founded in 1975, this college offers the following certificate programs:

+ Business Administration
+ Corrections
+ Environmental Science*
+ Office Services

It also offers degrees in the following areas:

+ Anishinaabe Studies
+ Business Administration
+ Early Childhood Education
+ Environmental Science*
+ Liberal Studies with Art or Criminal Justice Emphasis

Saginaw Chippewa Tribal College (Mount Pleasant, MI)

Founded in 1998, this college offers the following degrees, which are intended for transfer to a four-year university.

+ Associate of Arts in Liberal Arts
+ Associate of Arts in Native American Studies
+ Associate of Arts in Business

Minnesota

Fond du Lac Tribal and Community College (Cloquet, MN)

Founded in 1987, this college offers 10 certificate and diploma programs, as well as 15 degree programs, including Environmental Science.* It also has several community outreach programs, including an Environmental Institute, the St. Louis River Watch program, and a Tribal Earth Science & Technology program/

Leech Lake Tribal College (Cass Lake, MN)

Founded in 1990, this college has three academic divisions:
+ Arts & Humanities
+ Career & Technical Education
+ Science, Technology, Engineering, and Math*

White Earth Tribal and Community College (Mahnomen, MN)

Founded in 1997, this college offers one associate of arts degree, in Humanities, Arts, & Social Sciences.

Montana

Aaniiih Nakoda College (Harlem, MT)

Founded in 1984, this college offers four certificate programs, as well as the following degrees:
+ Associate of Arts (8 degrees)
+ Associate of Science (4 degrees)*
+ Associate of Applied Science (2 degrees)

Blackfeet Community College (Browning, MT)

Founded in 1974, this college offers associate degrees and certificates in six academic divisions:
+ Business & Information Technology
+ Education and Health
+ Humanities
+ Human Services

+ Math and Science
+ Nursing

Chief Dull Knife College (Lame Deer, MT)

Founded in 1975, this college offers certificate programs, AA and AS degrees in a variety of areas, and Associate in Applied Science in Administrative Assistant and Business Management.

Fort Peck Community College (Poplar, MT)

Founded in 1969, this college offers the following:
+ Associate of Arts (7 degrees)
+ Associate of Science (5 degrees)*
+ Associate of Applied Science (3 degrees)

Little Big Horn College (Crow Agency, MT)

Founded in 1980, this college offers the following programs:
+ Associate of Arts (5 degrees, plus individualized study)
+ AS (4 degrees)
+ One-year Certificates (7 areas)

Salish Kootenai College (Pablo, MT)

Founded in 1977, this college has 25 academic departments, including Forestry and Wildlife & Fisheries,* both of which offer a BS. Others are either a workforce certificate, certificate of completion, associate degree, bachelor degree, or some combination for each department.

Stone Child College (Box Elder, MT)

Founded in 1984, this college offers the following programs:
+ AA (12 degrees)*
+ AS (6 degrees)
+ BS in Elementary Education

Nebraska

Little Priest Tribal College (Winnebago, NE)

Founded in 1996, this college has seven academic programs:

- Business
- Early Childhood Education
- Native American Studies
- Indigenous Science – Environment*
- Indigenous Science – Health
- Interdisciplinary Studies
- Teacher Education

Nebraska Indian Community College (Macy, NE)

Founded in 1973, this college offers the following programs:

- AA (5 degrees)
- AS in General Science
- AAS in Carpentry (also available as a certificate)
- AA in Paraeducator Pre-teacher Education

New Mexico

Institute of American Indian Arts (Santa Fe, NM)

Founded in 1962, this institute has nine degree programs:

- Art History
- Business
- Cinematic Arts
- Creative Writing
- Creating Writing (MFA)
- Indigenous Studies
- Museum Studies
- Performing Arts
- Studio Arts

Navajo Technical College (Crownpoint, NM)

Founded in 1979, this college has seven academic departments and a graduate school:

+ School of Applied Technology
+ School of Arts and Humanities
+ School of Business and Education
+ School of Diné Studies
+ School of Engineering, Math, & Technology
+ School of Nursing
+ School of Science*

Southwestern Indian Polytechnic Institute (Albuquerque, NM)

Founded in 1971, this institute has 13 programs of study:

+ Accounting
+ Adult & Developmental Education
+ Business Administration
+ Computer-Aided Drafting and Design (CADD)
+ Culinary Arts
+ Early Childhood Education
+ Environmental Science*
+ Geospatial Information Technology
+ Liberal Arts
+ Natural Resources Management*
+ Network Management
+ Pre-engineering
+ Vision Care Technology

North Dakota

Cankdeska Cikana Community College (Fort Totten, ND)

Founded in 1970, this college offers three certificates and the following degrees:
+ AA (5 degrees)
+ AS (4 degrees, including Natural Resource Management*)
+ AAS (3 degrees)

Nueta Hidatsa Sahnish College (New Town, ND)

Founded in 1973, this college offers seven certificates and the following degrees:
+ Bachelor (3 degrees, including a BS in Environmental Science*)
+ Associate (10 degrees, including an AS in Environmental Science*)

Sitting Bull College (Fort Yates, ND)

Founded in 1973, this college offers 20 programs of study, including a BS and a Master's in Environmental Science.

Turtle Mountain Community College (Belcourt, ND)

Foundered in 1972, this college offers the following programs:
+ BS in Teacher Education
+ BA in Leadership and Management
+ AS in Natural Resource Management*
+ AA (2 degrees)
+ AAS (8 degrees)
+ 20 Certificates

United Tribes Technical College (Bismarck, ND)

Founded in 1969, this college offers 15 programs, including a degree in Environmental Science & Research.

South Dakota

Oglala Lakota College (Kyle, SD)

Founded in 1971, this college has 10 academic departments of study and a graduate school:

- General Education
- Business
- Education
- Foundational Studies
- Humanities/Social Sciences
- Lakota Studies
- Math, Science, Tech*
- Nursing
- Social Work
- Vocational Education

Sinte Gleska University (Rosebud, SD)

Founded in 1971, this university has 10 academic divisions of study:

- Arts & Sciences*
- Business
- Education
- Foundational Studies
- GP Art Institute
- Human Services
- Institute of Technologies
- Nursing
- Lakota Studies
- Adult Basic Education

Sisseton Wahpeton College (Sisseton, SD)

Founded in 1979, this college offers the following:

- AA (2 degrees)
- AS (5 degrees)
- AAS (4 degrees)
- Certificates (5 programs)
- Gainful Employment Certificates (3 programs)

Washington

Northwest Indian College (Bellingham, WA)

Founded in 1973, this college offers the following:
- Degrees (4 bachelor programs)
- Two-year programs (7 areas)
- Certificates
- Awards of Completion

Wisconsin

College of Menominee Nation (Keshana, WI)

Founded in 1993, this college offers five areas of study:
- General Education
- BA in Public Administration
- BS in Business Administration
- BS in Early Childhood/Middle Childhood Education
- Associate of Arts & Sciences, Pre-engineering

Lac Courte Oreilles Ojibwa Community College (Hayward, WI)

Founded in 1982, this college offers 13 academic programs:
- Agricultural & Natural Resource Management*
- Accounting
- AODA (Substance Abuse Councilor) Certificate
- Culinary Arts Certificate
- Human Services
- Liberal Arts
- Native American Art Certificate
- Native American Studies
- Native American Tribal Management Certificate
- Office Support Specialist Certificate
- Ojibwe Language Specialty Certificate
- Personal Care Worker Certificate
- Pre-nursing

Associate Status Colleges
Oklahoma
College of the Muscogee Nation (Okmulgee, OK)

Founded in 2004, this college has four associate degree and two certificate programs:
- Native American Studies
- Gaming
- Tribal Services
- Police Science
- Certificate in Gaming
- Certificate in Mvskoke Language Studies

Wyoming
Wind River Tribal College (Ethete, WY)

This college was founded in 1997. For details, see www.aihec.org/index.html

Index

NOTE: - *p* following a page number indicates a photo

About the Authors

A NGELOU EZEILO, founder and CEO of the Greening Youth Foundation, is a leading social entrepreneur. She was elected to the Ashoka Fellowship in 2016 and is a member of the National Center for Civil and Human Rights' Women in Solidarity Society and the board of the Atlanta Audubon Society. She is also an advisory board member for the Arabia Mountain National Heritage Area and Outdoor Afro and a member of the Steering Committee for the new Children's Wellbeing Initiative,  a network of 22 changemakers working together to promote children's well-being across the country. She splits her time between Atlanta, GA, and Victoria Island, Nigeria, with her husband and partner. www.gyfoundation.org

NICK CHILES is one of the nation's foremost chroniclers of African American life, culture, and celebrity. He is the author or co-author of 14 books, including three *New York Times* bestsellers he wrote with R&B icon Bobby Brown, civil rights leader Rev. Al Sharpton, and gospel legend Kirk Franklin. A graduate of Yale, he served as a newspaper reporter, magazine writer, and magazine and website editor-in-chief during his years in journalism, winning nearly 20 major awards, including a 1992 Pulitzer Prize as part of a *New York Newsday* team. He is also a college professor of journalism. He lives in Atlanta, GA.

A Note about the Publisher

NEW SOCIETY PUBLISHERS is an activist, solutions-oriented publisher focused on publishing books for a world of change. Our books offer tips, tools, and insights from leading experts in sustainable building, homesteading, climate change, environment, conscientious commerce, renewable energy, and more — positive solutions for troubled times.

We're proud to hold to the highest environmental and social standards of any publisher in North America. This is why some of our books might cost a little more. We think it's worth it!

- We print all our books in North America, never overseas
- All our books are printed on **100% post-consumer recycled paper,** processed chlorine free, with low-VOC vegetable-based inks (since 2002)*
- Our corporate structure is an innovative employee shareholder agreement, so we're one-third employee-owned (since 2015)
- We're carbon-neutral (since 2006)
- We're certified as a B Corporation (since 2016)

At New Society Publishers, we care deeply about *what* we publish — but also about *how* we do business.

Download our catalogue at https://newsociety.com/Our-Catalog, or for a printed copy please email info@newsocietypub.com or call 1-800-567-6772 ext 111.

New Society Publishers
ENVIRONMENTAL BENEFITS STATEMENT

*By using 100% post-consumer recycled paper vs. virgin paper stock, New Society Publishers saves the following resources:[1] (per every 5,000 copies printed)

27	Trees
2,407	Pounds of Solid Waste
2,649	Gallons of Water
3,455	Kilowatt Hours of Electricity
4,376	Pounds of Greenhouse Gases
19	Pounds of HAPs, VOCs, and AOX Combined
7	Cubic Yards of Landfill Space

[1]Environmental benefits are calculated based on research done by the Environmental Defense Fund and other members of the Paper Task Force who study the environmental impacts of the paper industry.

Certified
Ⓑ
Corporation

FSC
MIX
Paper from
responsible sources
www.fsc.org   FSC® C016245

new society
PUBLISHERS
www.newsociety.com